Goldsmith's comedy has retained its freshness of wit, cleverness of plot manipulation, and sheer humanity for almost two hundred years. Few readers can resist the engaging rascality of Tony Lumpkin, the studied archness of Kate Hardcastle, the bumbling geniality of her parents, or the confused gallantry of her sometimes tongue-tied lover. The story rushes along with breathless hilarity as cases of mistaken identity trip over each other on-stage.

This is an Enriched Edition of *She Stoops to Conquer*. A special Reader's Supplement, appearing in the center insert, provides the following sections which have been designed to enhance understanding and deepen appreciation:

> *Biographical Background* • *Historical Background* • *Pictorial Background* (illustrations depicting dress, interiors, and manners of the period) • *Critical Excerpts* (samples of critical reaction to the play and the dramatist)

The editor for this edition was Harry Shefter, Professor of English, New York University. The contributing editor was Oscar H. Fidell.

SHE
STOOPS
TO CONQUER

or,

The Mistakes

of a Night

by

Oliver Goldsmith

WASHINGTON SQUARE PRESS
POCKET BOOKS • NEW YORK

SHE STOOPS TO CONQUER

WASHINGTON SQUARE PRESS edition published November, 1972

Published by
POCKET BOOKS, a division of Simon & Schuster, Inc.,
630 Fifth Avenue, New York, N.Y.

L

WASHINGTON SQUARE PRESS editions are distributed
in the U.S. by Simon & Schuster, Inc., 630 Fifth Avenue,
New York, N.Y. 10020 and in Canada by Simon & Schuster of Canada, Ltd., Richmond Hill, Ontario, Canada.

Standard Book Number: 671-46592-9.

Acknowledgments

"She stooped to conquer" and "A bashful young Englishman—1700's."
From *English Costume of the Eighteenth Century* by Iris Brooke and
James Laver. Reprinted by permission of the publishers, A. & C. Black
Ltd., London.

"Interior of English mansion—1700's." From *The English Interior* 1500—
1900 by Ralph Dutton. Reprinted by permission of the publishers, B. T.
Batsford Ltd., London.

"Interior of an English pub (from a painting by John Collet, 1750)."
From *Inside the Pub* by M. Gorham and H. McG. Dunett, with drawings
by Gordon Cullen. Reprinted by permission of the publishers, The Archi-
tectural Press, London.

"English post-chaise." From *Country Life*. Reprinted by permission.

"Decorative Screen—England—1700's." Courtesy of Parke-Bernet Galleries,
Inc.

To Samuel Johnson, L.L.D.

Dear Sir,

By inscribing this slight performance to you, I do not mean so much to compliment you as myself. It may do me some honor to inform the public, that I have lived many years in intimacy with you. It may serve the interests of mankind also to inform them, that the greatest wit may be found in a character, without impairing the most unaffected piety.

I have, particularly, reason to thank you for your partiality to this performance. The undertaking a comedy, not merely sentimental, was very dangerous; and **Mr. Colman,** who saw this piece in its various stages, always thought it so. However, I ventured to trust it to the public; and though it was necessarily delayed till late in the season, I have every reason to be grateful.

> I am, Dear Sir,
> Your most sincere friend,
> And admirer,
> Oliver Goldsmith.

George Colman (1732–1794): English dramatist, manager of Covent Garden Theater, and producer of Goldsmith's play

She Stoops to Conquer
or, The Mistakes of a Night

Characters

SIR CHARLES MARLOW

YOUNG MARLOW, HIS SON

HARDCASTLE

HASTINGS

TONY LUMPKIN

DIGGORY

MRS. HARDCASTLE

MISS HARDCASTLE

MISS NEVILLE

MAID

LANDLORD, SERVANTS, *etc.*

Please note that, in the text of the play, words for which there is a footnote have been printed in **boldface roman** type and words worthy of vocabulary study have been printed in ***boldface italics***.

The Editors

SHE STOOPS TO CONQUER

ACT I

Prologue

By David Garrick, *Esq.*

Enter Mr. Woodward, *dressed in black, and hold-
ing a handkerchief to his eyes.*

Excuse me, sirs, I pray—I can't yet speak—
   I'm crying now—and have been all the week!
"'Tis not alone this mourning suit," good masters;
   "I've that **within**"—for which there are no plasters!
Pray would you know the reason why I'm crying?
   The **Comic Muse,** long sick, is now a-dying!
And if she goes, my tears will never stop;
   For as a player, I can't squeeze out one drop:
I am undone, that's all—shall lose my bread—
   I'd rather, but that's nothing—lose my head.
When the sweet maid is laid upon the bier,
   Shuter and I shall be chief mourners here.

David Garrick (1717–1779): considered the greatest
English actor of his time; playwright, co-owner, and co-
manager of the Drury Lane Theater
   Mr. Woodward: a popular comedy actor of the day
   within: the expression is a paraphrase of lines from
Hamlet, Act I, Scene ii, ll. 77 *et seq.*
   Comic Muse: in mythology, Thalia, the inspiration
for comedy
   Shuter: Edward ("Ned") Shuter, the low-comedy
actor who took the part of Mr. Hardcastle

To her a *mawkish drab* of spurious breed,
 Who deal in sentimentals will succeed!
Poor Ned and I are dead to all intents;
 We can as soon speak Greek as **sentiments**.
Both nervous grown, to keep our spirits up,
 We now and then take down a hearty cup.
What shall we do?—If Comedy forsake us!
 They'll turn us out, and no one else will take us.
But, why can't I be moral?—Let me try—
 My heart thus pressing—fixed my face and eye—
With a **sententious** look, that nothing means
 (Faces are blocks, in sentimental scenes),
Thus I begin—"All is not gold that glitters,
 Pleasure seems sweet, but proves a glass of bitters.
When ign'rance enters, folly is at hand;
 Learning is better far than house and land.
Let not your virtue trip, who trips may stumble,
 And virtue is not virtue, if she tumble."
I give it up—morals won't do for me;
 To make you laugh, I must play tragedy.
One hope remains—hearing the **maid** was ill,
 A **doctor** comes this night to show his skill.
To cheer her heart, and give your muscles motion,
 He in five **draughts** prepared, presents a potion:

---

sentiments: the artificial feelings of the earlier style of playwriting against which Goldsmith rebelled
sententious: filled with pithy, moralized sayings
maid: that is, the muse of comedy
doctor: referring to Goldsmith both as a physician and a dramatist
draughts: acts of the play

A kind of magic charm—for be assured,
  If you will swallow it, the maid is cured.
But desp'rate the doctor, and her case is,
  If you reject the dose, and make wry faces!
This truth he boasts, will boast it while he lives,
  No pois'nous drugs are mixed in what he gives.
Should he succeed, you'll give him his degree;
  If not, **within** he will receive no fee!
The college, you, must his pretensions back,
  Pronounce him regular, or dub him quack.

---

within: If the doctor doesn't succeed, he gets no fee
or reward.

ACT I

Scene I: A chamber in an old-fashioned house.

Enter Mrs. Hardcastle *and* Mr. Hardcastle.

MRS. HARDCASTLE. I vow, Mr. Hardcastle, you're very particular. Is there a creature in the whole country, but ourselves, that does not take a trip to town now and then, to rub off the rust a little? There's the two Miss Hoggs, and our neighbor, Mrs. Grigsby, go to take a month's polishing every winter.

HARDCASTLE. Aye, and bring back vanity and affectation to last them the whole year. I wonder why London cannot keep its own fools at home. In my time, the follies of the town crept slowly among us, but now they travel faster than a stagecoach. Its *fopperies* come down, not only as inside passengers, but in the very **basket**.

MRS. HARDCASTLE. Aye, *your* times were fine times, indeed; you have been telling us of *them* for many a long year. Here we live in an old rumbling mansion, that looks for all the world like an **inn**, but that we never see company. Our best visitors are old Mrs. Oddfish, the curate's wife, and little

---

basket: the large baggage compartment behind the coach which was sometimes used for extra passengers

Cripplegate, the lame dancing master: and all our entertainment your old stories of **Prince Eugene** and the **Duke of Marlborough.** I hate such old-fashioned trumpery.

HARDCASTLE. And I love it. I love everything that's old: old friends, old times, old manners, old books, old wine; and, I believe, Dorothy (*taking her hand*), you'll own I have been pretty fond of an old wife.

MRS. HARDCASTLE. Lord, Mr. Hardcastle, you're forever at your Dorothy's and your old wife's. You may be a **Darby,** but I'll be no **Joan,** I promise you. I'm not so old as you'd make me, by more than one good year. Add twenty to twenty, and make money of that.

HARDCASTLE. Let me see; twenty added to twenty makes just fifty and seven.

MRS. HARDCASTLE. It's false, Mr. Hardcastle: I was but twenty when I was brought to bed of Tony, that I had by Mr. Lumpkin, my first husband; and he's not come to years of discretion yet.

HARDCASTLE. Nor ever will, I dare answer for him. Aye, you have taught *him* finely!

MRS. HARDCASTLE. No matter. Tony Lumpkin has a good fortune. My son is not to live by his learning. I don't think a boy wants much learning to spend fifteen hundred a year.

Prince Eugene (1663–1736): Prince of Savoy and Austrian general, and the **Duke of Marlborough** (1650–1722), who was John Churchill, commanded the Austrian and English forces against the French in the War of the Spanish Succession

Darby and **Joan:** a proverbial, loving old couple who appear in a poem *The Happy Old Couple*

HARDCASTLE. Learning, **quotha!** A mere composition of tricks and mischief!

MRS. HARDCASTLE. Humor, my dear; nothing but humor. Come, Mr. Hardcastle, you must allow the boy a little humor.

HARDCASTLE. I'd sooner allow him a horsepond! If burning the footmen's shoes, frightening the maids, and worrying the kittens be humor, he has it. It was but yesterday he fastened my wig to the back of my chair, and when I went to make a bow, I popped my bald head in Mrs. Frizzle's face!

MRS. HARDCASTLE. And am I to blame? The poor boy was always too sickly to do any good. A school would be his death. When he comes to be a little stronger, who knows what a year or two's Latin may do for him?

HARDCASTLE. Latin for him! A cat and fiddle! No, no, the alehouse and the stable are the only schools he'll ever go to.

MRS. HARDCASTLE. Well, we must not snub the poor boy now, for I believe we shan't have him long among us. Anybody that looks in his face may see he's consumptive.

HARDCASTLE. Aye, if growing too fat be one of the symptoms.

MRS. HARDCASTLE. He coughs sometimes.

HARDCASTLE. Yes, when his liquor goes the wrong way.

MRS. HARDCASTLE. I'm actually afraid of his lungs.

HARDCASTLE. And truly, so am I; for he sometimes

---

quotha: an old-fashioned expression for "she says"

whoops like a speaking trumpet—(Tony *hallooing behind the scenes*) O, there he goes—a very consumptive figure, truly!

Enter Tony, *crossing the stage.*

MRS. HARDCASTLE. Tony, where are you going, my charmer? Won't you give papa and I a little of your company, lovee?

TONY. I'm in haste, mother; I cannot stay.

MRS. HARDCASTLE. You shan't venture out this raw evening, my dear; you look most shockingly.

TONY. I can't stay, I tell you. The Three Pigeons expects me down every moment. There's some fun going forward.

HARDCASTLE. Aye; the alehouse, the old place: I thought so.

MRS. HARDCASTLE. A low, paltry set of fellows.

TONY. Not so low, neither. There's Dick Muggins, the exciseman; Jack Slang the horse doctor; Little Aminadab, that grinds the music box; and Tom Twist, that spins the pewter platter.

MRS. HARDCASTLE. Pray, my dear, disappoint them for one night at least.

TONY. As for disappointing *them,* I should not so much mind; but I can't abide to disappoint *myself.*

MRS. HARDCASTLE (*detaining him*). You shan't go.

TONY. I will, I tell you.

MRS. HARDCASTLE. I say you shan't.

TONY. We'll see which is strongest, you or I.

Exit, hauling her out.

---

exciseman: tax collector

Hardcastle **solus.**

HARDCASTLE. Aye, there goes a pair that only spoil each other. But is not the whole age in a combination to drive sense and discretion out of doors? There's my pretty darling Kate; the fashions of the times have almost infected her too. By living a year or two in town, she is as fond of gauze and French **frippery** as the best of them.

Enter Miss Hardcastle.

HARDCASTLE. Blessings on my pretty innocence! Dressed out as usual, my Kate. Goodness! What a quantity of superfluous silk hast thou got about thee, girl! I could never teach the fools of this age that the indigent world could be clothed out of the trimmings of the vain.

MISS HARDCASTLE. You know our agreement, sir. You allow me the morning to receive and pay visits, and to dress in my own manner; and in the evening I put on my housewife's dress to please you.

HARDCASTLE. Well, remember, I insist on the terms of our agreement; and, by the bye, I believe I shall have occasion to try your obedience this very evening.

MISS HARDCASTLE. I protest, sir, I don't comprehend your meaning.

HARDCASTLE. Then to be plain with you, Kate, I expect the young gentleman I have chosen to be your husband from town this very day. I have his

---

solus: alone, by himself
frippery: showy display

father's letter, in which he informs me his son is set out, and that he intends to follow himself shortly after.

MISS HARDCASTLE. Indeed! I wish I had known something of this before. Bless me, how shall I behave? It's a thousand to one I shan't like him; our meeting will be so formal, and so like a thing of business, that I shall find no room for friendship or esteem.

HARDCASTLE. Depend upon it, child, I'll never control your choice; but Mr. Marlow, whom I have pitched upon, is the son of my old friend, Sir Charles Marlow, of whom you have heard me talk so often. The young gentleman has been bred a scholar, and is designed for an employment in the service of his country. I am told he's a man of an excellent understanding.

MISS HARDCASTLE. Is he?

HARDCASTLE. Very generous.

MISS HARDCASTLE. I believe I shall like him.

HARDCASTLE. Young and brave.

MISS HARDCASTLE. I'm sure I shall like him.

HARDCASTLE. And very handsome.

MISS HARDCASTLE. My dear papa, say no more *(kissing his hand)*. He's mine, I'll have him!

HARDCASTLE. And, to crown all, Kate, he's one of the most bashful and reserved young fellows in all the world.

MISS HARDCASTLE. Eh! you have frozen me to death again. That word "reserved" has undone all the rest of his accomplishments. A reserved lover, it is said, always makes a suspicious husband.

HARDCASTLE. On the contrary, modesty seldom resides in a breast that is not enriched with nobler virtues. It was the very feature in his character that first struck me.

MISS HARDCASTLE. He must have more striking features to catch me, I promise you. However, if he be so young, so handsome, and so everything as you mention, I believe he'll do still. I think I'll have him.

HARDCASTLE. Aye, Kate, but there is still an obstacle. It is more than an even wager, he may not have *you.*

MISS HARDCASTLE. My dear papa, why will you mortify one so? Well, if he refuses, instead of breaking my heart at his indifference, I'll only break my glass for its flattery, set my cap to some newer fashion, and look out for some less difficult admirer.

HARDCASTLE. Bravely resolved! In the meantime I'll go prepare the servants for his reception; as we seldom see company, they want as much training as a company of recruits the first day's **muster.**

Exit.

MISS HARDCASTLE (*sola*). Lud, this news of papa's puts me all in a flutter. Young, handsome; these he put last; but I put them foremost. Sensible, good-natured; I like all that. But then reserved, and sheepish; that's much against him. Yet can't he be cured of his timidity by being taught to be proud of his wife? Yes, and can't I—but I vow I'm disposing of the husband before I have secured the lover.

---

muster: assembly, collection

Enter Miss Neville.

MISS HARDCASTLE. I'm glad you're come, Neville, my dear. Tell me, Constance, how do I look this evening? Is there anything whimsical about me? Is it one of my well-looking days, child? Am I in face today?

MISS NEVILLE. Perfectly, my dear. Yet, now I look again—bless me!—sure, no accident has happened among the canary birds or the goldfishes? Has your brother or the cat been meddling? Or has the last novel been too moving?

MISS HARDCASTLE. No; nothing of all this. I have been threatened—I can scarce get it out—I have been threatened with a lover.

MISS NEVILLE. And his name?

MISS HARDCASTLE. Is Marlow.

MISS NEVILLE. Indeed!

MISS HARDCASTLE. The son of Sir Charles Marlow.

MISS NEVILLE. As I live, the most intimate friend of Mr. Hastings, *my* admirer. They are never **asunder.** I believe you must have seen him when we lived in town.

MISS HARDCASTLE. Never.

MISS NEVILLE. He's a very singular character, I assure you. Among women of reputation and virtue, he is the modestest man alive; but his acquaintance give him a very different character among creatures of another stamp: you understand me.

---

asunder: apart, separate

MISS HARDCASTLE. An odd character, indeed. I shall never be able to manage him. What shall I do? Pshaw, think no more of him, but trust to occurrences for success. But how goes on your own affair, my dear? Has my mother been courting you for my brother Tony as usual?

MISS NEVILLE. I have just come from one of our agreeable tête-à-têtes. She has been saying a hundred tender things, and setting off her pretty monster as the very pink of perfection.

MISS HARDCASTLE. And her partiality is such that she actually thinks him so. A fortune like yours is no small temptation. Besides, as she has the sole management of it, I'm not surprised to see her unwilling to let it go out of the family.

MISS NEVILLE. A fortune like mine, which chiefly consists in jewels, is no such mighty temptation. But at any rate, if my dear Hastings be but constant, I make no doubt to be too hard for her at last. However, I let her suppose that I am in love with her son; and she never once dreams that my affections are fixed upon another.

MISS HARDCASTLE. My good brother holds out stoutly. I could almost love him for hating you so.

MISS NEVILLE. It is a good-natured creature at bottom, and I'm sure would wish to see me married to anybody but himself. But my aunt's bell rings for our afternoon's walk round the improvements. **Allons.** Courage is necessary, as our affairs are critical.

Allons: "Forward" or "let us go" in French

MISS HARDCASTLE. "Would it were bed-time and all were well." *Exeunt.*

Scene II: An alehouse room.

Several shabby fellows with punch and to-bacco. Tony at the head of the table, a little higher than the rest, a mallet in his hand.

Omnes. Hurrea! hurrea! hurrea! bravo!

FIRST FELLOW. Now, gentlemen, silence for a song. The squire is going to **knock himself down** for a song.

OMNES. Aye, a song, a song.

TONY. Then I'll sing you, gentlemen, a song I made upon this alehouse, the Three Pigeons.

Song

Let schoolmasters puzzle their brain
    With grammar, and nonsense, and learning;
Good liquor, I stoutly maintain,
    Gives genius a better discerning.

---

  well: Falstaff's words, approximately, to Hal in Shakespeare's *King Henry IV, Part I*, Act 5, scene i, l. 125
  Omnes: all, all together
  knock himself down: Tony himself will sing

Let them brag of their heathenish gods,
   Their **Lethes,** their **Styxes,** and **Stygians;**
Their **Quis,** and their **Quaes,** and their **Quods,**
   They're all but a parcel of **pigeons.**
                    Toroddle, toroddle, toroll!
When Methodist preachers come down,
   A-preaching that drinking is sinful,
I'll wager the rascals a crown,
   They always preach best with a skinful.
But when you come down with your pence,
   For a slice of their **scurvy** religion,
I'll leave it to all men of sense,
   But you, my good friend, are the pigeon.
                    Toroddle, toroddle, toroll!
Then come, put the **jorum** about,
   And let us be merry and clever,
Our hearts and our liquors are stout,
   Here's the Three Jolly Pigeons for ever.
Let some cry up woodcock or hare,
   Your **bustards,** your ducks, and your **widgeons;**
But of all the birds in the air,
   Here's a health to the Three Jolly Pigeons.
                    Toroddle, toroddle, toroll!

   Lethes, Styxes, Stygians: Greek mythological rivers
for forgetfulness, hate, and gloominess
   Quis, Quaes, Quods: Latin declensions of relative
pronouns. In spite of Tony's supposed ignorance, he
shows some familiarity with Latin.
   pigeons: a pun on the name of the inn. Learned
men, in Tony's opinion, are silly pigeons.
   scurvy: contemptible or mean
   jorum: a large drinking bowl
   bustards: cranelike birds
   widgeons: freshwater ducks

OMNES. Bravo, bravo!

FIRST FELLOW. The squire has got spunk in him.

SECOND FELLOW. I love to hear him sing, **bekeays** he never gives us nothing that's *low*.

THIRD FELLOW. O damn anything that's *low*, I cannot bear it.

FOURTH FELLOW. The genteel thing is the genteel thing at any time; if so be that a gentleman bees in a *concatenation* accordingly.

THIRD FELLOW. I like the **maxum** of it, Master Muggins. What, though I am obligated to dance a bear, a man may be a gentleman for all that. May this be my poison if my bear ever dances but to the very genteelest of tunes: **"Water Parted,"** or the minuet in **Ariadne.**

SECOND FELLOW. What a pity it is the squire is not come to his own. It would be well for all the **publicans** within ten miles round of him.

TONY. **Ecod,** and so it would, Master Slang. I'd then show what it was to keep choice of company.

SECOND FELLOW. Oh, he takes after his own father for that. To be sure, old squire Lumpkin was the finest gentleman I ever set my eyes on. For

---

bekeays: because

maxum: maxim or universal truth

"Water Parted": a song in an opera, *Artaxerxes*, by the English composer Thomas A. Arne (1710–1778)

Ariadne: The minuet was a dance in the overture to *Ariadne*, an operetta by George Frederick Handel (1685–1759).

publicans: innkeepers

Ecod: an obsolete exclamation, something like "Egad" or "Ye Gods!"

winding the straight horn, or beating a thicket for a hare, or a wench, he never had his fellow. It was a saying in the place, that he kept the best horses, dogs, and girls, in the whole county.

TONY. Ecod, and when I'm of age I'll be no bastard, I promise you. I have been thinking of Bet Bouncer and the miller's gray mare to begin with. But come, my boys, drink about and be merry, for you pay no reckoning. Well, Stingo, what's the matter?

Enter Landlord.

LANDLORD. There be two gentlemen in a post chaise at the door. They have lost their way upo' the forest; and they are talking something about Mr. Hardcastle.

TONY. As sure as can be, one of them must be the gentleman that's coming down to court my sister. Do they seem to be Londoners?

LANDLORD. I believe they may. They look **woundily** like Frenchmen.

TONY. Then desire them to step this way, and I'll set them right in a twinkling. (*Exit* Landlord.) Gentlemen, as they mayn't be good enough company for you, step down for a moment, and I'll be with you in the squeezing of a lemon.

Exeunt Mob.

TONY (*solus*). **Father-in-law** has been calling me

---

woundily: very much

Father-in-law: Tony means his stepfather, Mr. Hardcastle.

whelp and hound this half year. Now, if I pleased, I could be so revenged upon the old grumbletonian. But then I'm afraid—afraid of what? I shall soon be worth fifteen hundred a year, and let him frighten me out of *that* if he can!

Enter Landlord, *conducting* Marlow *and* Hastings.

MARLOW. What a tedious, uncomfortable day have we had of it! We were told it was but forty miles across the country, and we have come above threescore!

HASTINGS. And all, Marlow, from that unaccountable reserve of yours that would not let us enquire more frequently on the way.

MARLOW. I own, Hastings, I am unwilling to lay myself under an obligation to everyone I meet, and often stand the chance of an unmannerly answer.

HASTINGS. At present, however, we are not likely to receive any answer.

TONY. No offense, gentlemen. But I'm told you have been enquiring for one Mr. Hardcastle in these parts. Do you know what part of the country you are in?

HASTINGS. Not in the least, sir, but should thank you for information.

TONY. Nor the way you came?

HASTINGS. No, sir; but if you can inform us—

TONY. Why, gentlemen, if you know neither the road you are going, nor where you are, nor the road you came, the first thing I have to inform you is, that—you have lost your way.

MARLOW. We wanted no ghost to tell us **that.**

TONY. Pray, gentlemen, may I be so bold as to ask the place from whence you came?

MARLOW. That's not necessary towards directing us where we are to go.

TONY. No offense; but question for question is all fair, you know. Pray, gentlemen, is not this same Hardcastle a cross-grained, old-fashioned, whimsical fellow with an ugly face, a daughter, and a pretty son?

HASTINGS. We have not seen the gentleman; but he has the family you mention.

TONY. The daughter, a tall, trapesing, trolloping, talkative maypole—the son, a pretty, well-bred, agreeable youth, that everybody is fond of?

MARLOW. Our information differs in this. The daughter is said to be well-bred, and beautiful; the son, an awkward booby, reared up and spoiled at his mother's apron string.

TONY. He-he-hem!—Then, gentlemen, all I have to tell you is, that you won't reach Mr. Hardcastle's house this night, I believe.

HASTINGS. Unfortunate!

TONY. It's a damned long, dark, boggy, dirty, dangerous way. Stingo, tell the gentlemen the way to Mr. Hardcastle's. (*Winking upon the* Landlord.) Mr. Hardcastle's of Quagmire Marsh, you understand me.

LANDLORD. Master Hardcastle's! Lack-a-daisy, my

---

that: a reference to Horatio's comment in *Hamlet,* Act I, scene v, l. 125

masters, you're come a deadly deal wrong! When you came to the bottom of the hill, you should have crossed down Squash Lane.

MARLOW. Cross down Squash Lane!

LANDLORD. Then you were to keep straight forward, until you came to four roads.

MARLOW. Come to where four roads meet!

TONY. Aye, but you must be sure to take only one of them.

MARLOW. O, sir, you're facetious!

TONY. Then, keeping to the right, you are to go sideways till you come upon Crack-skull Common: there you must look sharp for the track of the wheel, and go forward, till you come to Farmer Murrain's barn. Coming to the farmer's barn, you are to turn to the right, and then to the left, and then to the right about again, till you find out the old mill—

MARLOW. Zounds, man! We could as soon find out the longitude!

HASTINGS. What's to be done, Marlow?

MARLOW. This house promises but a poor reception; though perhaps the landlord can accommodate us.

LANDLORD. Alack, master, we have but one spare bed in the whole house.

TONY. And to my knowledge, that's taken up by three lodgers already. (*After a pause, in which the rest seem disconcerted.*) I have hit it. Don't you think, Stingo, our landlady could accommodate the gentlemen by the fireside, with—three chairs and a *bolster?*

HASTINGS. I hate sleeping by the fireside.

MARLOW. And I detest your three chairs and a bolster.

TONY. You do, do you?—then let me see—what if you go on a mile further, to the Buck's Head; the old Buck's Head on the hill, one of the best inns in the whole country?

HASTINGS. Oho! so we have escaped an adventure for this night, however.

LANDLORD (*apart to* Tony). Sure, you ben't sending them to your father's as an inn, be you?

TONY. Mum, you fool, you. Let *them* find that out. (*To them.*) You have only to keep on straight forward, till you come to a large old house by the roadside. You'll see a pair of large horns over the door. That's the sign. Drive up the yard, and call stoutly about you.

HASTINGS. Sir, we are obliged to you. The servants can't miss the way?

TONY. No, no: but I tell you, though, the landlord is rich, and going to leave off business; so he wants to be thought a gentleman, saving your presence, he! he! he! He'll be for giving you his company, and, ecod, if you mind him, he'll persuade you that his mother was an alderman, and his aunt a justice of peace!

LANDLORD. A troublesome old blade, to be sure; but 'a keeps as good wines and beds as any in the whole country.

MARLOW. Well, if he supplies us with these, we shall want no further connection. We are to turn to the right, did you say?

TONY. No, no; straight forward. I'll just step myself, and show you a piece of the way. (*To the* Landlord.) Mum.

LANDLORD. Ah, bless your heart for a sweet, pleasant—damned mischievous son of a strumpet.

Exeunt.

SHE STOOPS TO CONQUER

ACT II

ACT II

An *old-fashioned house.*

(*Enter* Hardcastle, *followed by three or four awkward* Servants.)

HARDCASTLE. Well, I hope you're perfect in the table exercise I have been teaching you these three days. You all know your posts and your places, and can show that you have been used to good company, without ever stirring from home.

OMNES. Aye, aye.

HARDCASTLE. When company comes, you are not to pop out and stare, and then run in again, like frightened rabbits in a warren.

OMNES. No, no.

HARDCASTLE. You, Diggory, whom I have taken from the barn, are to make a show at the side table; and you, Roger, whom I have advanced from the plow, are to place yourself behind *my* chair. But you're not to stand so, with your hands in your pockets. Take your hands from your pockets, Roger; and from your head, you blockhead, you. See how

Diggory carries his hands. They're a little too stiff, indeed, but that's no great matter.

DIGGORY. Aye, mind how I hold them. I learned to hold my hands this way, when I was upon drill for the militia. And so being upon drill—

HARDCASTLE. You must not be so talkative, Diggory. You must be all attention to the guests. You must hear us talk, and not think of talking; you must see us drink, and not think of drinking; you must see us eat, and not think of eating.

DIGGORY. By the laws, your worship, that's parfectly unpossible. Whenever Diggory sees yeating going forward, ecod, he's always wishing for a mouthful himself.

HARDCASTLE. Blockhead! Is not a bellyful in the kitchen as good as a bellyful in the parlor? Stay your stomach with that reflection.

DIGGORY. Ecod, I thank your worship, I'll make a shift to stay my stomach with a slice of cold beef in the pantry.

HARDCASTLE. Diggory, you are too talkative. Then, if I happen to say a good thing, or tell a good story at table, you must not all burst out a-laughing, as if you made part of the company.

DIGGORY. Then, ecod, your worship must not tell the story of old Grouse in the gun room: I can't help laughing at that—he! he! he!—for the soul of me! We have laughed at that these twenty years— ha! ha! ha!

HARDCASTLE. Ha! ha! ha! The story is a good one. Well, honest Diggory, you may laugh at that—but still remember to be attentive. Suppose one of the company should call for a glass of wine, how will you behave? A glass of wine, sir, if you please. (*To* Diggory.) Eh, why don't you move?

DIGGORY. Ecod, your worship, I never have courage till I see the eatables and drinkables brought upo' the table, and then I'm as bauld as a lion.

HARDCASTLE. What, will nobody move?

FIRST SERVANT. I'm not to leave this pleace.

SECOND SERVANT. I'm sure it's no pleace of mine.

THIRD SERVANT. Nor mine, for sartain.

DIGGORY. Wauns, and I'm sure it canna be mine.

HARDCASTLE. You numskulls! and so while, like your betters, you are quarreling for places, the guests must be starved. O, you dunces! I find I must begin all over again.—But don't I hear a coach drive into the yard? To your posts, you blockheads. I'll go in the meantime and give my old friend's son a hearty reception at the gate.   *Exit* Hardcastle.

DIGGORY. **By the elevens,** my pleace is gone quite out of my head.

ROGER. I know that my pleace is to be everywhere!

FIRST SERVANT. Where the devil is mine?

SECOND SERVANT. My pleace is to be nowhere at all; and so I'ze go about my business!

Exeunt Servants, *running about as if frightened, different ways.*

By the elevens: an expression like "Heavens!" apparently coined by Goldsmith

Enter Servant *with candles, showing in* Marlow
and Hastings.

SERVANT. Welcome, gentlemen, very welcome!
This way.

HASTINGS. After the disappointments of the day,
welcome once more, Charles, to the comforts of a
clean room and a good fire. Upon my word, a very
well-looking house; antique but creditable.

MARLOW. The usual fate of a large mansion.
Having first ruined the master by good housekeep-
ing, it at last comes to levy contributions as an inn.

HASTINGS. As you say, we passengers are to be
taxed to pay for all these fineries. I have often seen
a good sideboard, or a marble chimney piece,
though not actually put in the bill, inflame a reckoning confoundedly.

MARLOW. Travelers, George, must pay in all
places. The only difference is, that in good inns you
pay dearly for luxuries, in bad inns, you are fleeced
and starved.

HASTINGS. You have lived pretty much among
them. In truth, I have been often surprised that you,
who have seen so much of the world, with your
natural good sense, and your many opportunities,
could never yet acquire a *requisite* share of assurance.

MARLOW. The Englishman's malady. But tell me,
George, where could I have learned that assurance
you talk of? My life has been chiefly spent in a
college or an inn, in seclusion from that lovely part

of the creation that chiefly teach men confidence. I don't know that I was ever familiarly acquainted with a single modest woman—except my mother. But among females of another class, you know—

HASTINGS. Aye, among them you are impudent enough of all conscience!

MARLOW. They are of *us*, you know.

HASTINGS. But in the company of women of reputation I never saw such an idiot, such a trembler; you look for all the world as if you wanted an opportunity of stealing out of the room.

MARLOW. Why, man, that's because I *do* want to steal out of the room. Faith, I have often formed a resolution to break the ice, and rattle away at any rate. But I don't know how, a single glance from a pair of fine eyes has totally overset my resolution. An impudent fellow may counterfeit modesty, but I'll be hanged if a modest man can ever counterfeit impudence.

HASTINGS. If you could but say half the fine things to them, that I have heard you lavish upon the barmaid of an inn, or even a college bed-maker—

MARLOW. Why, George, I can't say fine things to them. They freeze, they petrify me. They may talk of a comet, or a burning mountain, or some such bagatelle; but to me, a modest woman, dressed out in all her finery, is the most tremendous object of the whole creation.

HASTINGS. Ha! ha! ha! At this rate, man, how can you ever expect to marry?

MARLOW. Never; unless, as among kings and princes, my bride were to be courted by *proxy*.

If, indeed, like an Eastern bridegroom, one were
to be introduced to a wife he never saw before, it
might be endured. But to go through all the terrors
of a formal courtship, together with the episode of
aunts, grandmothers, and cousins, and at last to
blurt out the broad staring question of, Madam,
will you marry me? No, no, that's a strain much
above me, I assure you!

HASTINGS. I pity you. But how do you intend
behaving to the lady you are come down to visit at
the request of your father?

MARLOW. As I behave to all other ladies. Bow very
low; answer yes, or no, to all her demands. But for
the rest, I don't think I shall venture to look in her
face till I see my father's again.

HASTINGS. I'm surprised that one who is so warm
a friend can be so cool a lover.

MARLOW. To be *explicit,* my dear Hastings, my
chief inducement down was to be instrumental in
forwarding your happiness, not my own. Miss
Neville loves you; the family don't know you; as
my friend you are sure of a reception; and let honor
do the rest.

HASTINGS. My dear Marlow! But I'll suppress the
emotion. Were I a wretch, meanly seeking to carry
off a fortune, you should be the last man in the
world I would apply to for assistance. But Miss
Neville's person is all I ask, and that is mine, both
from her deceased father's consent, and her own
inclination.

MARLOW. Happy man! You have talents and art
to captivate any woman. I'm doomed to adore the

sex, and yet to converse with the only part of it I despise. This stammer in my address, and this awkward *unprepossessing* visage of mine, can never permit me to soar above the reach of a milliner's prentice, or one of the **duchesses of Drury Lane.** Pshaw! this fellow here to interrupt us.

Enter Hardcastle.

HARDCASTLE. Gentlemen, once more you are heartily welcome. Which is Mr. Marlow? Sir, you're heartily welcome. It's not my way, you see, to receive my friends with my back to the fire. I like to give them a hearty reception in the old style at my gate. I like to see their horses and trunks taken care of.

MARLOW *(aside)*. He has got our names from the servants already. *(To him.)* We approve your caution and hospitality, sir. *(To* Hastings.*)* I have been thinking, George, of changing our traveling dresses in the morning. I am grown confoundedly ashamed of mine.

HARDCASTLE. I beg, Mr. Marlow, you'll use no ceremony in this house.

HASTINGS. I fancy, [Charles], you're right: the first blow is half the battle. I intend opening the campaign with the white and gold.

HARDCASTLE. Mr. Marlow—Mr. Hastings—gentlemen—pray be under no constraint in this house.

---

duchesses of Drury Lane: loose, immoral women who frequented the theater district

This is Liberty Hall, gentlemen. You may do just as you please here.

MARLOW. Yet, George, if we open the campaign too fiercely at first, we may want ammunition before it is over. I think to reserve the embroidery to secure a retreat.

HARDCASTLE. Your talking of a retreat, Mr. Marlow, puts me in mind of the Duke of Marlborough, when we went to besiege **Denain.** He first summoned the garrison—

MARLOW. Don't you think the **ventre d'or** waistcoat will do with the plain brown?

HARDCASTLE. He first summoned the garrison, which might consist of about five thousand men—

HASTINGS. I think not: brown and yellow mix but very poorly.

HARDCASTLE. I say, gentlemen, as I was telling you, he summoned the garrison, which might consist of about five thousand men—

MARLOW. The girls like finery.

HARDCASTLE. Which might consist of about five thousand men, well appointed with stores, ammunition, and other implements of war. "Now," says the Duke of Marlborough to George Brooks, that stood next to him—you must have heard of George Brooks—"I'll pawn my Dukedom," says he, "but I take that garrison without spilling a drop of blood." So—

Denain: where the French defeated the Duke's forces in 1712

ventre d'or: literally, in French, "golden belly"— that is, a gold-colored vest

MARLOW. What, my good friend, if you gave us a glass of punch in the meantime, it would help us to carry on the siege with vigor.

HARDCASTLE. Punch, sir! *(Aside.)* This is the most unaccountable kind of modesty I ever met with.

MARLOW. Yes, sir, punch! A glass of warm punch, after our journey, will be comfortable. This is Liberty Hall, you know.

HARDCASTLE. Here's a cup, sir.

MARLOW *(aside)*. So this fellow, in his **Liberty Hall,** will only let us have just what he pleases.

HARDCASTLE *(taking the cup)*. I hope you'll find it to your mind. I have prepared it with my own hands, and I believe you'll own the ingredients are tolerable. Will you be so good as to pledge me, sir? Here, Mr. Marlow, here is our better acquaintance. *(Drinks.)*

MARLOW *(aside)*. A very impudent fellow this! But he's a character, and I'll humor him a little. Sir, my service to you. *(Drinks.)*

HASTINGS *(aside)*. I see this fellow wants to give us his company, and forgets that he's an innkeeper, before he has learned to be a gentleman.

MARLOW. From the excellence of your cup, my old friend, I suppose you have a good deal of business in this part of the country. Warm work, now and then, at elections, I suppose?

HARDCASTLE. No, sir, I have long given that work over. Since our betters have hit upon the **expedient**

Liberty Hall: a place of complete freedom
expedient: a compromise or practical method to achieve an end

of electing each other, there's no business **"for us that sell ale."**

HASTINGS. So, then you have no turn for politics, I find.

HARDCASTLE. Not in the least. There was a time, indeed, I fretted myself about the mistakes of government, like other people; but finding myself every day grow more angry, and the government growing no better, I left it to mend itself. Since that, I no more trouble my head about **Heyder Ally** or **Ally Cawn** than about **"Ally Croaker."** Sir, my service to you.

HASTINGS. So that with eating **above stairs,** and **drinking below,** with receiving your friends within, and amusing them without, you lead a good, pleasant, bustling life of it.

HARDCASTLE. I do stir about a great deal, that's certain. Half the differences of the parish are adjusted in this very parlor.

MARLOW (*after drinking*). And you have an argu-

"for us that sell ale": the common people—those that deal with or use ordinary, inexpensive drink, the group with whom Hardcastle now humorously identifies himself

Ally Croaker: a play upon the Indian title, "Ali." Heyder Ali was the real-life Sultan of Mysore and Ali Khan ("Cawn") was the Sultan of Bengal. "Ally Croaker" was the title of a well-known Irish tune.

above . . . below: In the private homes of the well-to-do, the servants went about their menial jobs in the basement or on the ground floor area, while their masters dined and lived in the upstairs rooms or quarters.

ment in your cup, old gentleman, better than any in **Westminster Hall.**

HARDCASTLE. Aye, young gentleman, that, and a little philosophy.

MARLOW *(aside)*. Well, this is the first time I ever heard of an innkeeper's philosophy.

HASTINGS. So then, like an experienced general, you attack them on every quarter. If you find their reason manageable, you attack it with your philosophy; if you find they have no reason, you attack them with this. Here's your health, my philosopher. *(Drinks.)*

HARDCASTLE. Good, very good, thank you; ha! ha! Your generalship puts me in mind of Prince Eugene, when he fought the Turks at the battle of Belgrade. You shall hear—

MARLOW. Instead of the battle of Belgrade, I believe it's almost time to talk about supper. What has your philosophy got in the house for supper?

HARDCASTLE. For supper, sir! *(Aside.)* Was ever such a request to a man in his own house!

MARLOW. Yes, sir, supper, sir; I begin to feel an appetite. I shall make devilish work tonight in the *larder*, I promise you.

HARDCASTLE *(aside)*. Such a brazen dog sure never my eyes beheld. *(To him.)* Why, really, sir, as for supper I can't well tell. My Dorothy, and the cook-maid, settle these things between them. I leave these kind of things entirely to them.

Westminster Hall: a law court in London

MARLOW. You do, do you?

HARDCASTLE. Entirely. By the bye, I believe they are in actual consultation upon what's for supper this moment in the kitchen.

MARLOW. Then I beg they'll admit *me* as one of their privy council. It's a way I have got. When I travel I always chose to regulate my own supper. Let the cook be called. No offense, I hope, sir.

HARDCASTLE. Oh no, sir, none in the least; yet, I don't know how: our Bridget, the cook-maid, is not very communicative upon these occasions. Should we send for her, she might scold us all out of the house.

HASTINGS. Let's see your list of the larder, then. I ask it as a favor. I always match my appetite to my bill of fare.

MARLOW (*to* Hardcastle, *who looks at them with surprise*). Sir, he's very right, and it's my way, too.

HARDCASTLE. Sir, you have a right to command here. Here, Roger, bring us the bill of fare for tonight's supper; I believe it's drawn out. [*Exit* Roger.] Your manner, Mr. Hastings, puts me in mind of my uncle, Colonel Wallop. It was a saying of his, that no man was sure of his supper till he had eaten it.

HASTINGS (*aside*). All upon the high ropes! His uncle a colonel! We shall soon hear of his mother being a justice of peace. [*Re-enter* Roger.] But let's hear the bill of fare.

MARLOW (*perusing*). What's here? For the first

course; for the second course; for the dessert. The devil, sir, do you think we have brought down the whole **Joiners' Company,** or the **Corporation of Bedford,** to eat up such a supper? Two or three little things, clean and comfortable, will do.

HASTINGS. But let's hear it.

MARLOW *(reading).* For the first course at the top, a pig, and prune sauce.

HASTINGS. Damn your pig, I say!

MARLOW. And damn your prune sauce, say I!

HARDCASTLE. And yet, gentlemen, to men that are hungry, pig with prune sauce is very good eating.

MARLOW. At the bottom a calf's tongue and brains.

HASTINGS. Let your brains be knocked out, my good sir, I don't like them.

MARLOW. Or you may clap them on a plate by themselves. I do.

HARDCASTLE *(aside).* Their impudence confounds me. *(To them.)* Gentlemen, you are my guests, make what alterations you please. Is there anything else you wish to retrench or alter, gentlemen?

MARLOW. Item: A pork pie, a boiled rabbit and sausages, a **florentine,** a **shaking pudding,** and a dish of **tiff-taff-taffety cream!**

Joiners' Company: a group of carpenters or wood-workers

Corporation of Bedford: officials of the City of Bedford

florentine: a baked meat pie; also a kind of chocolate cookie

shaking pudding: a jellylike pudding

tiff-taff-taffety cream: an old-fashioned cream dish

HASTINGS. Confound your made dishes; I shall be as much at a loss in this house as at a green and yellow dinner at the French ambassador's table. I'm for plain eating.

HARDCASTLE. I'm sorry, gentlemen, that I have nothing you like, but if there be anything you have a particular fancy to—

MARLOW. Why really, sir, your bill of fare is so exquisite, that any one part of it is full as good as another. Send us what you please. So much for supper. And now to see that our beds are aired, and properly taken care of.

HARDCASTLE. I entreat you'll leave all that to me. You shall not stir a step.

MARLOW. Leave that to you! I protest, sir, you must excuse me; I always look to these things myself.

HARDCASTLE. I must insist, sir, you'll make yourself easy on that head.

MARLOW. You see I'm resolved on it. *(Aside.)* A very troublesome fellow this, as ever I met with.

HARDCASTLE. Well, sir, I'm resolved at least to attend you. *(Aside.)* This may be modern modesty, but I never saw anything look so like old-fashioned impudence.

Exeunt Marlow *and* Hardcastle.

HASTINGS *(solus)*. So I find this fellow's civilities begin to grow troublesome. But who can be angry at those **assiduities** which are meant to please him? Ha! what do I see? Miss Neville, by all that's happy!

---

assiduities: devoted attentions

Enter Miss Neville.

MISS NEVILLE. My dear Hastings! To what unexpected good fortune, to what accident, am I to *ascribe* this happy meeting?

HASTINGS. Rather let me ask the same question, as I could never have hoped to meet my dearest Constance at an inn.

MISS NEVILLE. An inn! Sure you mistake; my aunt, my guardian, lives here. What could induce you to think this house an inn?

HASTINGS. My friend, Mr. Marlow, with whom I came down, and I, have been sent here as to an inn, I assure you. A young fellow, whom we accidentally met at a house hard by, directed us thither.

MISS NEVILLE. Certainly it must be one of my hopeful cousin's tricks, of whom you have heard me talk so often: ha! ha! ha!

HASTINGS. He whom your aunt intends for you? He of whom I have such just apprehensions?

MISS NEVILLE. You have nothing to fear from him, I assure you. You'd adore him if you knew how heartily he despises me. My aunt knows it, too, and has undertaken to court me for him, and actually begins to think she has made a conquest.

HASTINGS. Thou dear *dissembler!* You must know, my Constance, I have just seized this happy opportunity of my friend's visit here to get admittance into the family. The horses that carried us down are now fatigued with their journey, but they'll soon be refreshed; and then, if my dearest girl will

trust in her faithful Hastings, we shall soon be
landed in France, where even among slaves the
laws of marriage are respected.

MISS NEVILLE. I have often told you that though
ready to obey you, I yet should leave my little
fortune behind with reluctance. The greatest part of
it was left me by my uncle, the **India Director,**
and chiefly consists in jewels. I have been for some
time persuading my aunt to let me wear them. I
fancy I'm very near succeeding. The instant they
are put into my possession you shall find me ready
to make them and myself yours.

HASTINGS. Perish the baubles! Your person is all
I desire. In the meantime, my friend Marlow must
not be let into his mistake. I know the strange
reserve of his temper is such that, if abruptly in-
formed of it, he would instantly quit the house
before our plan was ripe for execution.

MISS NEVILLE. But how shall we keep him in the
deception? Miss Hardcastle is just returned from
walking; what if we still continue to deceive him?—
This, this way—(*They confer.*)

Enter Marlow.

MARLOW. The assiduities of these good people
tease me beyond bearing. My host seems to think it
ill manners to leave me alone, and so he claps not
only himself, but his old-fashioned wife on my

India Director: a director of the famous trading
company—the East India Company; in brief, a wealthy
man

back. They talk of coming to sup with us, too; and then, I suppose, we are to run the gantlet through all the rest of the family.—What have we got here?—

HASTINGS. My dear Charles! Let me congratulate you!—The most fortunate accident!—Who do you think is just alighted?

MARLOW. Cannot guess.

HASTINGS. Our mistresses, boy, Miss Hardcastle and Miss Neville. Give me leave to introduce Miss Constance Neville to your acquaintance. Happening to dine in the neighborhood, they called, on their return, to take fresh horses here. Miss Hardcastle has just stepped into the next room, and will be back in an instant. Wasn't it lucky? eh!

MARLOW (aside). I have just been mortified enough of all conscience, and here comes something to complete my embarrassment.

HASTINGS. Well! but wasn't it the most fortunate thing in the world?

MARLOW. Oh! yes. Very fortunate—a most joyful encounter.—But our dresses, George, you know, are in disorder.—What if we should postpone the happiness till tomorrow?—Tomorrow at her own house. —It will be every bit as convenient—and rather more respectful.—Tomorrow let it be. (Offering to go.)

MISS NEVILLE. By no means, sir. Your ceremony will displease her. The disorder of your dress will show the ardor of your impatience. Besides, she knows you are in the house, and will permit you to see her.

MARLOW. Oh! the devil! how shall I support it? Hem! hem! Hastings, you must not go. You are to assist me, you know. I shall be confoundedly ridiculous. Yet, hang it! I'll take courage. Hem!

HASTINGS. Pshaw, man! it's but the first plunge, and all's over. She's but a woman, you know.

MARLOW. And of all women, she that I dread most to encounter!

Enter Miss Hardcastle, *as returned from walking, a bonnet, etc.*

HASTINGS (*introducing them*). Miss Hardcastle. Mr. Marlow. I'm proud of bringing two persons of such merit together, that only want to know, to esteem each other.

MISS HARDCASTLE (*aside*). Now, for meeting my modest gentleman with a *demure* face, and quite in his own manner. (*After a pause, in which he appears very uneasy and disconcerted.*) I'm glad of your safe arrival, sir—I'm told you had some accidents by the way.

MARLOW. Only a few, madam. Yes, we had some. Yes, madam, a good many accidents, but should be sorry—madam—or rather glad of any accidents—that are so agreeably concluded. Hem!

HASTINGS (*to him*). You never spoke better in your whole life. Keep it up, and I'll insure you the victory.

MISS HARDCASTLE. I'm afraid you flatter, sir. You that have seen so much of the finest company can find little entertainment in an obscure corner of the country.

MARLOW *(gathering courage).* I have lived, indeed, in the world, madam; but I have kept very little company. I have been but an observer upon life, madam, while others were enjoying it.

MISS NEVILLE. But that, I am told, is the way to enjoy it at last.

HASTINGS *(to him).* Cicero never spoke better. Once more, and you are confirmed in assurance forever.

MARLOW *(to him).* Hem! Stand by me, then, and when I'm down, throw in a word or two to set me up again.

MISS HARDCASTLE. An observer, like you, upon life, were, I fear, disagreeably employed, since you must have had much more to censure than to approve.

MARLOW. Pardon me, madam. I was always willing to be amused. The folly of most people is rather an object of mirth than uneasiness.

HASTINGS *(to him).* Bravo, bravo. Never spoke so well in your whole life. Well, Miss Hardcastle, I see that you and Mr. Marlow are going to be very good company. I believe our being here will but embarrass the interview.

MARLOW. Not in the least, Mr. Hastings. We like your company of all things. *(To him.)* Zounds! George, sure you won't go? How can you leave us?

HASTINGS. Our presence will but spoil conversation, so we'll retire to the next room. *(To him.)* You don't consider, man, that we are to manage a little *tête-à-tête* of our own.

        Exeunt [Hastings *and* Miss Neville.]

MISS HARDCASTLE (*after a pause*). But you have not been wholly an observer, I presume, sir. The ladies, I should hope, have employed some part of your addresses.

MARLOW (*relapsing into timidity*). Pardon me, madam, I—I—I—as yet have studied—only—to—deserve them.

MISS HARDCASTLE. And that some say is the very worst way to obtain them.

MARLOW. Perhaps so, madam. But I love to converse only with the more grave and sensible part of the sex.—But I'm afraid I grow tiresome.

MISS HARDCASTLE. Not at all, sir; there is nothing I like so much as grave conversation myself; I could hear it forever. Indeed, I have often been surprised how a man of sentiment could ever admire those light airy pleasures, where nothing reaches the heart.

MARLOW. It's—a disease—of the mind, madam. In the variety of tastes there must be some who, wanting a relish for—um-a-um.

MISS HARDCASTLE. I understand you, sir. There must be some, who, **wanting** a relish for refined pleasures, pretend to despise what they are incapable of tasting.

MARLOW. My meaning, madam, but infinitely better expressed. And I can't help observing—a—

---

    wanting: lacking

Miss Hardcastle (*aside*). Who could ever suppose this fellow impudent upon some occasions. (*To him.*) You were going to observe, sir—

Marlow. I was observing, madam—I protest, madam, I forget what I was going to observe.

Miss Hardcastle (*aside*). I vow and so do I. (*To him.*) You were observing, sir, that in this age of hypocrisy—something about hypocrisy, sir.

Marlow. Yes, madam. In this age of hypocrisy, there are few who upon strict inquiry do not—a—a—a—

Miss Hardcastle. I understand you perfectly, sir.

Marlow (*aside*). Egad! and that's more than I do myself!

Miss Hardcastle. You mean that in this hypocritical age there are few that do not condemn in public what they practise in private, and think they pay every debt to virtue when they praise it.

Marlow. True, madam; those who have most virtue in their mouths, have least of it in their bosoms. But I'm sure I tire you, madam.

Miss Hardcastle. Not in the least, sir; there's something so agreeable and spirited in your manner, such life and force—pray, sir, go on.

Marlow. Yes, madam. I was saying—that there are some occasions—when a total want of courage, madam, destroys all the—and puts us—upon a—a—a—

Miss Hardcastle. I agree with you entirely, a want of courage upon some occasions assumes the appearance of ignorance, and betrays us when we most want to excel. I beg you'll proceed.

MARLOW. Yes, madam. Morally speaking, madam —but I see Miss Neville expecting us in the next room. I would not intrude for the world.

MISS HARDCASTLE. I protest, sir, I never was more agreeably entertained in all my life. Pray go on.

MARLOW. Yes, madam. I was—but she beckons us to join her. Madam, shall I do myself the honor to attend you?

MISS HARDCASTLE. Well then, I'll follow.

MARLOW (aside). This pretty smooth dialogue has done for me.   *Exit.*

MISS HARDCASTLE (sola). Ha! ha! ha! Was there ever such a sober, sentimental interview? I'm certain he scarce looked in my face the whole time. Yet the fellow, but for his unaccountable bashfulness, is pretty well, too. He has good sense, but then so buried in his fears, that it fatigues one more than ignorance. If I could teach him a little confidence, it would be doing somebody that I know of a piece of service. But who is that somebody?— That, faith, is a question I can scarce answer. *Exit.*

Enter Tony *and* Miss Neville, *followed by* Mrs. Hardcastle *and* Hastings.

TONY. What do you follow me for, cousin Con? I wonder you're not ashamed to be so very engaging.

MISS NEVILLE. I hope, cousin, one may speak to one's own relations, and not be to blame.

TONY. Aye, but I know what sort of a relation you

want to make me, though; but it won't do. I tell you, cousin Con, it won't do; so I beg you'll keep your distance, I want no nearer relationship. *(She follows, coquetting him to the back scene.)*

Mrs. Hardcastle. Well! I vow, Mr. Hastings, you are very entertaining. There's nothing in the world I love to talk of so much as London, and the fashions, though I was never there myself.

Hastings. Never there! You amaze me! From your air and manner, I concluded you had been bred all your life either at Ranelagh, St. James's, or **Tower Wharf.**

Mrs. Hardcastle. Oh! sir, you're only pleased to say so. We country persons can have no manner at all. I'm in love with the town, and that serves to raise me above some of our neighboring rustics; but who can have a manner, that has never seen the Pantheon, the Grotto Gardens, the Borough, and such places where the nobility chiefly resort? All I can do is to enjoy London at second hand. I take care to know every **tête-à-tête** from the *Scandalous*

Tower Wharf: Hastings is poking fun at Mrs. Hardcastle, who is unfamiliar with the geography of London. He mentions Tower Wharf, a disreputable section, in the same breath as Ranelagh and St. James's, fashionable resorts of the nobility, but she doesn't know the difference. Similarly, he speaks of the Grotto Gardens in the Borough of Southwark as if it were as elegant as the Pantheon.

tête-à-tête: This was a portrait or sketch of society figures involved in a scandalous situation. Magazines like the publication noted here, as well as *The Town and Country Magazine,* printed short biographies appealing to a gossip-hungry audience.

Magazine, and have all the fashions as they come out, in a letter from the two Miss Rickets of Crooked Lane. Pray how do you like this **head,** Mr. Hastings?

HASTINGS. Extremely elegant and **dégagée,** upon my word, madam. Your **friseur** is a Frenchman, I suppose?

MRS. HARDCASTLE. I protest, I dressed it myself from a print in the *Ladies' Memorandum-book* for the last year.

HASTINGS. Indeed. Such a head in a side box, at the playhouse, would draw as many gazers as my Lady Mayoress at a city ball.

MRS. HARDCASTLE. I vow, since inoculation began, there is no such thing to be seen as a **plain woman;** so one must dress a little particular, or one may escape in the crowd.

HASTINGS. But that can never be your case, madam, in any dress! *(Bowing.)*

MRS. HARDCASTLE. Yet, what signifies *my* dressing when I have such a piece of antiquity by my side as Mr. Hardcastle? All I can say will never argue down a single button from his clothes. I have often wanted him to throw off his great flaxen wig, and

---

head: a style of hairdress; a wig on a wire frame affected by fashionable ladies

dégagée: casual; "in the know." Hastings is purposely flattering Mrs. Hardcastle by assuming that she understands French.

friseur: hairdresser

plain woman: a woman made unattractive because of marks left on her face by smallpox. Thanks to inoculation introduced to England in 1718 by Lady Mary Wortley Montagu, such disfigurement became infrequent.

where he was bald, to plaster it over like my Lord Pately, with powder.

Hastings. You are right, madam; for, as among the ladies there are none ugly, so among the men there are none old.

Mrs. Hardcastle. But what do you think his answer was? Why, with his usual Gothic vivacity, he said I only wanted him to throw off his wig to convert it into a **tête** for my own wearing!

Hastings. Intolerable! At your age you may wear what you please, and it must become you.

Mrs. Hardcastle. Pray, Mr. Hastings, what do you take to be the most fashionable age about town?

Hastings. Some time ago forty was all the mode; but I'm told the ladies intend to bring up fifty for the ensuing winter.

Mrs. Hardcastle. Seriously? Then I shall be too young for the fashion!

Hastings. No lady begins now to put on jewels till she's past forty. For instance, Miss there, in a polite circle would be considered as a child, as a mere maker of samplers.

Mrs. Hardcastle. And yet **Mrs.** Niece thinks herself as much a woman, and is as fond of jewels as the oldest of us all.

Hastings. Your niece, is she? And that young gentleman, a brother of yours, I should presume?

Mrs. Hardcastle. My son, sir. They are con-

---

tête: a wig (literally, a "head" in French)

Mrs.: a term of address (mistress) formerly used also for unmarried, respectable females

tracted to each other. Observe their little sports. They fall in and out ten times a day, as if they were man and wife already. *(To them.)* Well, Tony, child, what soft things are you saying to your cousin Constance this evening?

Tony. I have been saying no soft things; but that it's very hard to be followed about so! Ecod! I've not a place in the house now that's left to myself but the stable.

Mrs. Hardcastle. Never mind him, Con, my dear. He's in another story behind your back.

Miss Neville. There's something generous in my cousin's manner. He falls out before faces to be forgiven in private.

Tony. That's a damned confounded—**crack.**

Mrs. Hardcastle. Ah! he's a sly one. Don't you think they're like each other about the mouth, Mr. Hastings? The Blenkinsop mouth to a *T.* They're of a size, too. Back to back, my pretties, that Mr. Hastings may see you. Come, Tony.

Tony. You had as good not make me, I tell you. *(Measuring.)*

Miss Neville. Oh lud! he has almost cracked my head.

Mrs. Hardcastle. Oh, the monster! For shame, Tony. You a man, and behave so!

Tony. If I'm a man, let me have my fortin. Ecod! I'll not be made a fool of no longer.

Mrs. Hardcastle. Is this, ungrateful boy, all that I'm to get for the pains I have taken in your educa-

---

crack: untrue remark

tion? I that have rocked you in your cradle, and fed that pretty mouth with a spoon! Did not I work that *waistcoat* to make you genteel? Did not I prescribe for you every day, and weep while the receipt was operating?

Tony. Ecod! you had reason to weep, for you have been dosing me ever since I was born. I have gone through every receipt in *The Complete Housewife* ten times over; and you have thoughts of coursing me through **Quincy** next spring. But, ecod! I tell you, I'll not be made a fool of no longer.

Mrs. Hardcastle. Wasn't it all for your good, viper? Wasn't it all for your good?

Tony. I wish you'd let me and my good alone, then. Snubbing this way when I'm in spirits. If I'm to have any good, let it come of itself; not to keep dinging it, dinging it into one so.

Mrs. Hardcastle. That's false; I never see you when you're in spirits. No, Tony, you then go to the alehouse or kennel. I'm never to be delighted with your agreeable wild notes, unfeeling monster!

Tony. Ecod! Mamma, your own notes are the wildest of the two.

Mrs. Hardcastle. Was ever the like? But I see he wants to break my heart, I see he does.

Hastings. Dear Madam, permit me to lecture the

Quincy: Dr. John Quincy was the author of the *Complete English Dispensatory*, a popular book listing home medications ("receipts") to be used by housewives. Tony pretends to be fearful that his mother will try these remedies on him as well as the ones she had already tried on him from *The Complete Housewife*.

young gentleman a little. I'm certain I can persuade him to his duty.

MRS. HARDCASTLE. Well, I must retire. Come, Constance, my love. You see, Mr. Hastings, the wretchedness of my situation. Was ever poor woman so plagued with a dear, sweet, pretty, provoking, undutiful boy?

Exeunt Mrs. Hardcastle *and* Miss Neville.

Hastings, Tony

TONY (*singing*). "There was a young man riding by, and fain would have his will. Rang do didlo dee."
Don't mind her. Let her cry. It's the comfort of her heart. I have seen her and sister cry over a book for an hour together, and they said they liked the book the better the more it made them cry.

HASTINGS. Then you're no friend to the ladies, I find, my pretty young gentleman?

TONY. That's as I find 'um.

HASTINGS. Not to her of your mother's choosing, I dare answer! And yet she appears to me a pretty, well-tempered girl.

TONY. That's because you don't know her as well as I. Ecod! I know every inch about her; and there's not a more bitter *cantankerous* toad in all Christendom!

HASTINGS (*aside*). Pretty encouragement this for a lover!

TONY. I have seen her since the height of that.

She has as many tricks as a hare in a thicket, or a colt the first day's breaking.

HASTINGS. To me she appears sensible and silent.

TONY. Aye, before company. But when she's with her playmates, she's as loud as a hog in a gate.

HASTINGS. But there is a meek modesty about her that charms me.

TONY. Yes, but curb her never so little, she kicks up, and you're flung in a ditch.

HASTINGS. Well, but you must allow her a little beauty.—Yes, you must allow her some beauty.

TONY. Bandbox! She's all a made-up thing, mun. Ah! could you but see Bet Bouncer of these parts, you might then talk of beauty. Ecod, she has two eyes as black as sloes, and cheeks as broad and red as a pulpit cushion. She'd make two of she.

HASTINGS. Well, what say you of a friend that would take this bitter bargain off your hands?

TONY. Anon?

HASTINGS. Would you thank him that would take Miss Neville, and leave you to happiness and your dear Betsy?

TONY. Aye; but where is there such a friend, for who would take *her*?

HASTINGS. I am he. If you but assist me, I'll engage to whip her off to France, and you shall never hear more of her.

TONY. Assist you! Ecod, I will, to the last drop of my blood. I'll clap a pair of horses to your chaise that shall *trundle* you off in a twinkling, and may

---

Anon: used in the sense of "What did you say or mean?"

be get you a part of her fortin beside in jewels that you little dream of.

HASTINGS. My dear squire, this looks like a lad of spirit.

TONY. Come along then, and you shall see more of my spirit before you have done with me.
(*Singing.*)

> We are the boys
> That fears no noise
> Where the thundering cannons roar.

Exeunt.

SHE STOOPS
TO
CONQUER

—• •—

ACT III

SHE STOOPS TO CONQUER

OLIVER GOLDSMITH (1728–1774)

BIOGRAPHICAL BACKGROUND

It is unlikely that an author can avoid the inclusion of autobiographical material in his work. Oliver Goldsmith (1728–1774) was no exception to this practice and, indeed, there are incidents and characterizations in the play which derive from events in his own life. These real-life references enrich the robust comedy of *She Stoops to Conquer* and help to make human beings out of the actors.

Take, for example, the basic situation which provides the motivation of the play—Marlow's mistake in assuming that the country home of the Hardcastles is an inn. On pages 20T–24T, Marlow lets Tony know that he is lost and Tony tells him how to get to the "inn" of Mr. Hardcastle. Goldsmith was involved in a parallel situation, according to some biographers, when he was sixteen years old and was returning from Edgeworthstown, Ireland, playing the gentleman with some money in his pocket and riding on a hired horse. He stopped for the night at Ardagh to ask for the best inn. A prankster like Tony directed him to the mansion of a Mr. Featherstone who, unlike Mr. Hardcastle, was aware of Goldsmith's identity at once and, being a man of humor, "went along with the gag." Like Marlow who made a fuss about supper (pp. 38B–40T), Goldsmith did the same thing, going even further in ordering special dishes for his breakfast. When he learned of the deception, again like Marlow who felt like "a silly puppy" (p. 87B), Goldsmith was extremely upset and embarrassed.

Many other traits of Goldsmith's are reflected in Marlow's behavior. Goldsmith, poor and not particularly

Note: The page references above and on the following pages direct your attention to passages in the text (T for Top of page, M for Middle, and B for Bottom).

handsome, liked finery. Marlow, too, is very much concerned with dress. Marlow speaks of embroidery, a *ventre d'or* waistcoat, and of color combinations (p. 34T–B). He is also preoccupied with food, drink, putting on airs, and living like a "swell." Goldsmith had little female companionship in his life and longed for love and affection. Marlow says on page 31T, "I don't know that I was ever familiarly acquainted with a single modest woman—except my mother." Goldsmith was apparently awkward in the presence of fine ladies. So was Marlow—as he confesses on page 31M. Like young Goldsmith, who spent most of his time away from home, Marlow tells Hastings that his life has been mostly spent in a college or inn (p. 30B).

Marlow is not the only character through whom we glimpse scenes from Goldsmith's life. Tony Lumpkin, strangely, is another one; he reveals Goldsmith's own love for earthly pleasure. "I was a lover of mirth, good-humor and . . . fun from my childhood," said Goldsmith. Washington Irving tells us that Goldsmith "sang a good song, was a boon companion, and could not resist any temptation to social enjoyment." Evidence of these statements is obvious on pages 16T–19T. Goldsmith frequented an inn at Ballymahon, Ireland, where his rustic friends seem to have been the prototypes of Tony Lumpkin's companions described on page 10M. Furthermore, it is believed that Tony's drinking song (pp. 16B–17B) is a re-creation of a folksong popular in Ballymahon. Although Goldsmith, unlike Tony, had formal education, he believed with Tony that learning and dullness often went hand in hand, and when Tony sings "Good liquor . . . gives genius a better discerning" (p. 16B), Tony was only echoing the author's feelings.

Goldsmith, however, had the affection of a wider audience than Tony had, so wide in fact that William Makepeace Thackeray said of him, "Who, of the millions whom he has amused, does not love him? To be the most beloved of English writers, what a title that is for a man!" Unfortunately, during his lifetime, Goldsmith experienced few of the joys that come with renown and security.

He was born in poverty in County Longford, Ireland, in 1728, and died at forty-six, destitute in London. Smallpox disfigured his face early in life, and he grew up ugly, short, and ungraceful. Occasionally he revealed the agonizing sensitivity which he felt about his appearance because he was secretly vain, wearing gaudy raiment, including a peach-blossom coat, when he managed to get some fine clothes to set off his homely person.

His father was an Anglican clergyman who could not afford to send his son to college and, although Goldsmith himself almost became a clergyman, Washington Irving suggests that one reason that Goldsmith objected to clerical life (although he was rejected anyway as a clergyman) was that he would have to wear a black coat and clerical garb.

Thanks to his constant benefactor (his Uncle Thomas Contarine) and his getting a position as a "sizar"—a needy scholar who earned his keep at college by performing menial chores—he was sent to Trinity College, Dublin, at the age of seventeen. There he was constantly taunted and humiliated by the staff and the students, but he still kept his cheerfulness and animation, and was generous all his life even to the point of literally giving the shirt off his back or the blanket from his bed to people needier than he. Yet he continued to suffer wrong, this special wrong being, according to Thomas De Quincey, the fact that "he was never fully appreciated by any one friend . . . and he was always overshadowed by men less . . . genial, though more showy than himself."

Not brilliant in his early schooling, he hated mathematics, ethics, and logic, but loved the classics. He made many false starts in settling on a career, even trying out for law and apparently studying medicine at the University of Edinburgh. Abandoning for a time his medical career, Goldsmith instead roamed about Europe, learned to gamble and to be careless in money matters. In fact, he seems to have gotten into financial embarrassment largely because of his generous impulses in money matters. Part of this period of his life appears disguised in the novel, *The Vicar of Wakefield* (1766). However, he also seems to have acquired an M.D. degree, possibly in Padua or Louvain, and he began to practice medicine in London in 1756, but he failed as a physician.

About this time he took stock of himself and, despite his usual optimism and guileless simplicity, he confessed in a letter to his brother that "I am not that strong, active man you once knew me. You scarcely can conceive how much . . . disappointment, anguish and study have worn me down . . . I can neither laugh nor drink; have contracted a hesitating, disagreeable manner of speaking, and a visage that looks like ill nature itself . . . I say that books teach us very little of the world . . . teach your son . . . thrift and economy. Let his poor wandering uncle's example be placed before his eyes. I have learned from books to be disinterested and generous, before I was taught from experience the necessity of being prudent." But he did not follow his own advice!

After a brief period of working as an usher in a school, he turned to hack writing for several magazines and book publishers. The writing of two long poems, *The Traveler* (1764) and *The Deserted Village* (1770), as well as the production of his play, *The Good-Natured Man* (1768), earned for Goldsmith considerable wealth, which he spent heedlessly. Often he had no money for a night's lodging. Thomas Macaulay sorrowfully noted that "his heart was soft even to weakness: he was so generous, that he quite forgot to be just; he forgave injuries so readily, that he might be said to invite them, and was so liberal to beggars, that he had nothing left for his tailor and butcher."

The rise in Goldsmith's fortunes did not last very long. In 1773 came the triumphant *She Stoops to Conquer,* and, a few months later, the worn-out, misunderstood, and misguided writer of richly descriptive poetry, a sweetly sentimental novel, and robustly humorous plays was laid to rest.

HISTORICAL BACKGROUND

Living her quiet, rural life, Mrs. Hardcastle in *She Stoops to Conquer* glamorized London society of the middle and late 1700's as she wistfully spoke of it to Hastings (pp. 49T–50B). She longed for entertainment places like Vauxhall, Ranelagh, and the Pantheon and for the glitter of the town where nobility as well as would-be socialites paraded in fashionable dress along Pall Mall and St. James's Street. There, as Alvin Redman tells us, they dressed in magnificent style—"in ermine, satins, and brocades . . . exquisitely embroidered with gold or silver thread . . . the gentlemen vied with their ladies in the fantastic display of ostentatious fashion [while] manners were rigid and morals were lax."

Mrs. Hardcastle complained (p. 49B) that all she could do was "enjoy London at second hand." She followed eagerly all the gossip of the coffeehouses and took care to know every intimate detail about the socialites in the *Scandalous Magazine*. But this same society in its elegance and luxury cared little about the poverty of the non-aristocratic six or seven million other people in Britain. They were more interested in small talk, scandalizing, drinking, and gambling than they were in trade, agriculture, the professions, the church, or the state. They seemed to care just as little about the 800,000 people immediately around them in London, which was a city where public executions were frequently regarded as entertainment and where crime and violence flourished. Momentous changes in British life, such as the tremendous growth of the middle class and the development of industry and commerce, were occurring, but no hint of these changes appears in *She Stoops to Conquer*. No echoes of the difficulties with the American Colonies nor of scientific progress by such Englishmen as Priestley, Cavendish, Dalton, and others are heard.

For that matter neither did the Hardcastle family, country gentry, seem to concern itself in the play with eighteenth-century farming concepts which were changing, such as the enclosure system, i.e., the practice of fencing in fields and pastures formerly available for common cultivation and grazing. Perhaps Mr. Hardcastle would have fought the system if for no other reason than that it disturbed the old which he so dearly loved (p. 8T): "old friends, old times, old manners," etc. Goldsmith himself, of course, had given some recognition to the changes in the agricultural society in another work, *The Deserted Village.*

Goldsmith also believed some changes were needed in the world of the theater. He criticized the day's sentimental comedy—comedy in which, he said, "the virtues of private life are exhibited rather than vices exposed . . . in these plays, almost all the characters are good and exceedingly generous . . . folly, instead of being ridiculed, is commended, and the comedy aims at touching on passions, without the power of being truly pathetic. Humor at present seems to be departing from the stage." He thought comedy should be treated differently than in the usual sentimental way, and he wanted real-life pictures, true characters, and touches of humor. Apparently agreeing in this, the actor-theater manager, David Garrick, who wrote the prologue to *She Stoops to Conquer,* noted (p. 3M):

> "Pray would you know the reason why I'm crying?
> The Comic Muse, long sick, is now a-dying!"

The usual sentimental comedy of the period involved not real, natural feeling but the artificial, sophisticated reactions of society. Goldsmith's type of comedy was a little different from that of his contemporaries because he attempted to entertain honestly and to make people laugh by exaggerating nature and depending on the ridiculous. Audiences in his time were accustomed to look for "wit" instead of humor.

It may have been a reservation about Goldsmith's kind of humor as well as general hostility toward him by producer George Colman, with whom he had had some difficulty with his earlier play, *The Good-Natured Man*, that delayed the appearance of *She Stoops to Conquer* for two years. It first appeared at the Covent Garden Theatre on March 15, 1773. There had been some question about its title; friends of Goldsmith's encouraged him to call it *The Belle's Stratagem*—but Goldsmith insisted on paraphrasing a line of poetry by John Dryden whom he admired, the line being: "But kneels to conquer, and but stoops to rise." Samuel Johnson helped Goldsmith launch the play and even attracted a kind of claque to view the play at its opening performance.

She Stoops to Conquer earned about five hundred pounds for Goldsmith (which he promptly used to pay some of his debts) and would have earned even more for him if he hadn't given up the copyright to the play to a creditor. Goldsmith considered it a successful play because it made people laugh. Posterity has considered it so also because it still makes theatergoers laugh every time it is presented today—even in Esperanto.

FEATURES OF THE AUTHOR'S STYLE

Two words which often occur to readers of Goldsmith's lines are "charm" and "geniality." These terms are probably traceable, according to Ralph M. Wardle, to Goldsmith's desire to please all men, but such qualities could not have been communicated without an accompanying sharpness of mind which marks Goldsmith's style.

In *She Stoops to Conquer,* Goldsmith says clearly, quickly, and easily what he wants to say. He once noted that "the art of writing . . . is but another name for good sense." He didn't believe that he had to observe the principles of the classical writers nor those of his contemporaries. "He insisted that writers should strive for simplicity, should speak to all men," Wardle reminds us, and "he was interested in the affairs of simple, unsophisticated people . . . as individuals . . . in their emotions . . . he wanted more to touch their hearts, to gladden them, to make them laugh."

She Stoops to Conquer shows this philosophy. His characters in the play are not too complicated, yet they are not necessarily of the stock variety. As a matter of fact, Goldsmith is frequently credited with introducing two new kinds of characters: Mrs. Hardcastle and her son, Tony Lumpkin. They are fairly simple types; neither has any real malice despite their harassment of each other. Their actions are calculated to give a feeling of innocent merriment.

Goldsmith's language is straightforward and understandable, not forced. It may be sprinkled with some *I vow's* and *ecod's,* but it is easily followed by modern readers. Even when Mrs. Hardcastle is putting on airs, she speaks plainly as in her mild protest (p. 49B) that "we country persons can have no manner at all. I'm in love with the town, and that serves to raise me above some of our neighboring rustics; but who can have a manner, that has never seen the Pantheon, the Grotto Gardens, the Borough, and such places where the nobility chiefly resort?" This doesn't mean that Goldsmith couldn't on occasion use formal, stylistic devices in his writing for special effects, along with the best of his contemporaries. Witness his use of aphorism, a pithy sentence or maxim, such as Kate's pronouncement that "A reserved lover . . . makes a suspicious husband" (p. 12B) or Marlow's comment about travelers (p. 30M); his use of irony as in the pious statement of the alehouse carouser (p. 18T) who virtuously declares that he cannot *bear* anything *low;* or his easy handling of antithesis or parallel syntax (p. 120T). The use of these devices, however, in no way interferes with the understanding and enjoyment of the play.

Occasionally, the farce may appear broad, but Goldsmith's main intent was simply to provide laughter without driving home moralistic aspects of human behavior and to poke a little fun at the artificial refinement of eighteenth-century playwrights. What if the plot is a little improbable and we are asked to accept Tony's coach ride down Featherbed Lane forty miles away to Mrs. Hardcastle's backyard or the juggling of Constance Neville's jewels? The comic effect is the important thing and the events in the plot certainly supply it. Goldsmith's technique depended on exaggerating the actions of human beings and nature for the purposes of stressing the ludicrous. He achieved these purposes admirably, and to such an extent that J. Lobban was led to declare that the one great writer whose prose style Samuel Johnson could not eclipse was Oliver Goldsmith.

CHARACTER ANALYSIS

Even with the passage of almost two hundred years, the
people in *She Stoops to Conquer* have been characterized
by a modern critic as being full of juicy vitality. And so
they are.

"Hardcastle is a good-natured, particular old fellow,
fond of telling a story and ridiculous, without offending,"
Stephen Gwynn points out, "while Mr. Marlow [is] a man
of sense, education and breeding; but as many men are,
exceedingly timid in the presence of modest women . . .
though impudently familiar in company with those of
low degree. . . . The Squire [Tony] is a compound of
whim and good-natured mischief . . . Mrs. Dorothy Hardcastle, a foolishly fond mother and no bad wife. Miss
Hardcastle, a sensible lovely girl, full of spirit and good
humor. Miss Neville and Mr. Hastings, two very affectionate and enterprising lovers."

Old Hardcastle looks to the past (p. 8M), teases his
wife about her age, and sees through Tony, his stepson
(p. 9M), yet he is a shrewd parent in dealing with his
daughter Kate (pp. 11M–12T). He has come to terms
with the modern generation. He is a lovable bore when
he insists on retelling anecdotes about his old military days
at the siege of Denain (p. 34T) and a scolding master
when he coaches his servants (pp. 27B–29B), and yet
we are not offended by his actions. Even when he loses
patience with Marlow, who has treated him as a sub-
servient landlord, we are not annoyed by him because we
realize that in a similar situation we would probably have
been more short-tempered than he is.

Marlow we recognize as a sensitive and shy fellow.
When his friend Hastings criticizes him for his lack of
poise with ladies, Marlow almost pathetically explains

(pp. 30B–31T) that he has known only one modest woman—his mother—and that he finds the prospect of courting a fine lady terrifying (p. 32T). His bashfulness and his stammering are attributable to his early environment which he has never outgrown—weaknesses from which Goldsmith himself suffered. When Kate poses as a barmaid, however, he is a lion. He is a real lady killer on pages 73B–74T, immodestly boasting that he can't see what the ladies in London "find in me to follow." His real sensitivity and modesty become apparent when he realizes (pp. 87B–88T) that he has been hoaxed. "What a silly puppy do I find myself," he says in genuine chagrin to Kate, who is so impressed with his sincerity that she is more than ever eager not to let him go. "I never knew half his merit till now," she says on page 89M. Marlow is then determined, like a true gentleman, to "atone for the levity of my past conduct" on page 115B.

Kate is, of course, very sensible, spirited, and almost nonsentimental. She knows how to hang on to a good thing when she has one; she is determined to marry Marlow. She "stoops" in her guise as a comely barmaid and wins as a grand lady. There is no clinging-vine air about her, nor is there any hypocrisy. Although she may seem tomboyish in the opening scenes, she proves she is feminine and able in husband-catching. She changes her behavior quickly and skillfully; on pages 69B–70T she shows off her barmaid's costume to the maid and reveals herself as a cultured theatergoer, yet she switches her speech to that of an uneducated barmaid when she talks to Marlow in her "obstropalous manner" (p. 73M).

Constance Neville may be very affectionate toward her lover, Hastings, but she does not overlook the importance of money, despite her romantic view of love. ". . . though ready to obey you, I yet should leave my little fortune behind with reluctance" (p. 42T), she informs Hastings in discussing her aunt's possession of her jewels. Furthermore, we learn on page 113T that "In the moment of passion, fortune may be despised but it ever produces a lasting repentance."

Mrs. Hardcastle is a loving wife but, like many middle-aged women, she is reluctant to let go of her youth. She chides her husband for believing that she is older than she says she is (p. 8B) and acts coquettishly when Hastings praises her for her fashionable, youthful appearance (pp. 49M, 50T–51M). Vainly but forgivingly, she proclaims that she takes "care to know every tête-à-tête from the *Scandalous Magazine*" and that she follows all the new London fashions. Her hairdress is in the latest high style. When the tactful Hastings tells her that "the most fashionable age about town" is near fifty, she beams that she is "too young for the fashion!" and when he pretends to mistake her son Tony for her brother, she is delighted. She preens herself with Constance's jewelry and can be foolish and easily misled. Doting on her rascal of a son, Tony, she doesn't see any need for him to be learned "to spend fifteen hundred a year" (p. 8B), petulantly scolds him for not staying home with her to look after his health (p. 10M), and in general takes poorly disguised abuse from him. True, she does flare up at him when she realizes what a fool he has made of her in the wild-goose coach ride and in the matter of the jewels, but we do not feel any punishment will come to him because of her embarrassment since Tony is above all scolding.

After all, Tony is the real engineer of the plot. He has become a stock type of character since his creation by Goldsmith—part country bumpkin, buffoon, and practical joker, carousing with alehouse friends. But this "sheepish, mischievous, idle, cunning lout," as E. C. Brewer calls him, is not quite as simple as he seems, even with "the vices of a man and the frolics of a boy." He is self-indulgent and doesn't care to disappoint himself (p. 10B). "Let schoolmasters puzzle their brain/With grammar, and nonsense, and learning;/Good liquor . . . Gives genius a better discerning" he maintains on page 16B. His uneducated speech includes such expressions as "curb her never so little" (p. 55T), "fortin" for "fortune" (p. 63T), and "circumbendibus" (p. 107B), but he is very literate in such dialogues as his analysis of Constance Neville's actions on page 95T and his renouncement of her on page 119M. He is clever enough to "tell off" Hastings on page 108T and to point out correctly to his mother on page 112T that "you have spoiled me, and so you may take the fruits on't." He does not blame his little court of drinking friends for having spoiled him in any way. These lesser characters in the play, incidentally, are patterned after real-life rustics whom Goldsmith met in an inn in Ballymahon, Ireland, near his cousin's house.

PICTORIAL BACKGROUND

Mrs. Hardcastle. *Aye,* your *times were fine times, indeed; you have been telling us of* them *for many a long year. Here we live in an old rumbling mansion, that looks for all the world like an inn, but that we never see company. Our best visitors are old Mrs. Oddfish, the curate's wife, and little Cripplegate, the lame dancing master. . . . (p. 7B)*

INTERIOR OF ENGLISH MANSION—1700's

Hardcastle. *Blessings on my pretty innocence! Dressed out as usual, my Kate. Goodness! What a quantity of superfluous silk hast thou got about thee, girl! . . .*

Miss Hardcastle. *You know our agreement, sir. You allow me the morning . . . to dress in my own manner; and in the evening I put on my housewife's dress to please you. (p. 11M)*

ENGLISHWOMAN IN "SUPERFLUOUS SILK"—1700's

Miss Hardcastle. *I have been threatened—I can scarce get it out—I have been threatened with a lover.*

Miss Neville. *And his name?*

Miss Hardcastle. *Is Marlow.*

Miss Neville. *Indeed!*

Miss Hardcastle. *The son of Sir Charles Marlow. (p. 14M)*

ENGLISH GIRLS DISCUSSING THEIR FAVORITE SUBJECT

Omnes. *Hurrea! hurrea! hurrea! bravo!*

First Fellow. *Now, gentlemen, silence for a song. The squire is going to knock himself down for a song.*

' Omnes. *Aye, a song, a song.*

Tony. *Then I'll sing you, gentlemen, a song I made upon this alehouse, the Three Pigeons. (p. 16M)*

INTERIOR OF AN ENGLISH PUB
(FROM A PAINTING BY JOHN COLLET, 1750)

Tony. *He-he-hem!—Then, gentlemen, all I have to tell you is, that you won't reach Mr. Hardcastle's house this night, I believe.*

Hastings. *Unfortunate!*

Tony. *It's a damned long, dark, boggy, dirty, dangerous way.* (p. 21M)

TONY BEGINS HIS SLY GAME.
(Illustration by C. Morten—1800's)

Hastings. *But in the company of women of reputation I never saw such an idiot, such a trembler; you look for all the world as if you wanted an opportunity of stealing out of the room.* (p. 31T)

Marlow. *Why, man, that's because I* do *want to steal out of the room.* (p. 31T)

A BASHFUL YOUNG ENGLISHMAN–1700's

Hardcastle. *Mr. Marlow—Mr. Hastings—gentlemen—pray be under no constraint in this house. This is Liberty Hall, gentlemen. You may do just as you please here.*

Marlow. *Yet, George, if we open the campaign too fiercely at first, we may want ammunition before it is over.* (p. 33B)

ENGLISH GENTLEMEN—1700's

Marlow. *Instead of the battle of Belgrade, I believe it's almost time to talk about supper. What has your philosophy got in the house for supper?*

Hardcastle. *For supper, sir!* (Aside.) *Was ever such a request to a man in his own house!*

Marlow. *Yes, sir, supper, sir; I begin to feel an appetite.*
(p. 37M)

AN INDIGNANT ENGLISH GENTLEMAN

Marlow (reading). *For the first course at the top, a pig, and prune sauce.*

Hastings. *Damn your pig, I say!*

Marlow. *And damn your prune sauce, say I!*

Hardcastle. *And yet, gentlemen, to men that are hungry, pig with prune sauce is very good eating.* (p. 39T)

MARLOW AND HASTINGS BAIT THE "INNKEEPER."
(An old book illustration)

Miss Hardcastle. . . . *I'm glad of your safe arrival, sir—I'm told you had some accidents by the way.*

Marlow. *Only a few, madam. Yes, we had some. Yes, madam, a good many accidents, but should be sorry—madam —or rather glad of any accidents—that are so agreeably concluded. Hem!* (p. 44M)

THE BASHFUL SUITOR MEETS A LADY.
(Illustration by C. Morten—1800's)

Tony. *What do you follow me for, cousin Con? I wonder you're not ashamed to be so very engaging.*

Miss Neville. *I hope, cousin, one may speak to one's own relations, and not be to blame.*

Tony. *Aye, but I know what sort of a relation you want to make me; but it won't do . . . (p. 48B)*

TONY BEING HIS USUAL DIFFICULT SELF
(Illustration by C. Morten—1800's)

Miss Neville. *Oh lud! he has almost cracked my head.*

Mrs. Hardcastle. *Oh, the monster! For shame, Tony. You a man and behave so!*

Tony. *If I'm a man, let me have my fortin. Ecod! I'll not be made a fool of no longer. (p. 52B)*

TONY AND CONSTANCE BUMP HEADS.
(E. A. Abbey—1883)

Miss Hardcastle. *Mr. Marlow's . . . his timidity, struck me at the first sight.*

Hardcastle. *Then your first sight deceived you; for I think him one of the most brazen first sights that ever astonished my senses!*

Miss Hardcastle. *Sure, sir, you rally! I never saw anyone so modest.* (p. 60B)

FATHER AND DAUGHTER COMPARE NOTES ON MARLOW
(Illustration by E. A. Abbey—1883)

Mrs. Hardcastle. *Don't be alarmed, Constance. If they be lost, I must restore an equivalent. But my son knows they are missing, and not to be found.*

Tony. *That I can bear witness to. They are missing, and not to be found, I'll take my oath on't.* (p. 66M)

TONY TELLS A STRANGE TRUTH.
(Illustration by T. Cobb—1800's)

Miss Hardcastle. *Did your honor call?* . . .

Marlow. *No, child.* . . .

Miss Hardcastle. *Perhaps the other gentleman called, sir?* . . .

Marlow. *No, no, I tell you.* (Looks full in her face.) *Yes, child, I think I did call. I wanted—I wanted—I vow, child, you are vastly handsome.* (p. 71M)

A GENTLEMAN AND A MAID

Hardcastle. *Zounds! He'll drive me distracted if I contain myself any longer. Mr. Marlow, sir; I have submitted to your insolence for more than four hours, and I see no likelihood of its coming to an end. I'm now resolved to be master here, sir, and I desire that you and your drunken pack may leave my house directly.* (p. 84M)

MR. HARDCASTLE REACHES HIS LIMIT OF ENDURANCE.
(Illustration by E. A. Abbey—1883)

Marlow (aside). *By heavens, she weeps. This is the first mark of tenderness I ever had from a modest woman, and it touches me.* (To her.) *Excuse me, my lovely girl, you are the only part of the family I leave with reluctance. But . . . the difference of our birth, fortune and education, make an honorable connection impossible . . .* (p. 88M)

MARLOW IS TOUCHED BY THE "SIMPLE" MAID'S MODESTY.
(Illustration by E. A. Abbey—1883)

Tony. *Aye, you may steal for yourselves the next time. I have done my duty. She has got the jewels again, that's a sure thing; but she believes it was all a mistake of the servants.*

Miss Neville. *But, my dear cousin, sure, you won't forsake us in this distress. (p. 89B)*

MISS NEVILLE PLEADS WITH TONY.
(Illustration by E. A. Abbey—1883)

Diggory. *Where's the squire? I have got a letter for your worship.*

Tony. *Give it to my mamma. She reads all my letters first. . . .*

Miss Neville (aside). *Undone, undone. A letter to him from Hastings. I know the hand. If my aunt sees it, we are ruined forever. . . . (p. 91B)*

CONTROVERSY OVER A LETTER

Hastings. *You saw the old lady and Miss Neville drive off, you say?*

Servant. *Yes, your honor. They went off in a post coach, and the young squire went on horseback. They're thirty miles off by this time.*

Hastings. *Then all my hopes are over. (p. 101T)*

ENGLISH POST-CHAISE

Hardcastle. *Ha! ha! ha! The peremptory tone in which he sent forth his sublime commands.*

Sir Charles. *And the reserve with which I suppose he treated all your advances.*

Hardcastle. *And yet he might have seen something in me above a common innkeeper, too. (p. 101B)*

TWO ELDERLY GENTLEMEN IN PLEASANT DISCOURSE

Tony. *By my guess we should be upon Crackskull Common, about forty miles from home.*

Mrs. Hardcastle. *O lud! O lud! the most notorious spot in all the country. We only want a robbery to make a complete night on't.*

Tony. *Don't be afraid, mamma, don't be afraid. . . .*

(p. 109T)

LADY SURRENDERS HER PURSE TO A HIGHWAYMAN
(WHAT MRS. HARDCASTLE THOUGHT MIGHT HAPPEN!)

Mrs. Hardcastle (running forward from behind). *O lud, he'll murder my poor boy, my darling. Here, good gentleman, whet your rage upon me. Take my money, my life, but spare that young gentleman, spare my child, if you have any mercy.*

Hardcastle. *My wife! as I'm a Christian. (p. 111M)*

MRS. HARDCASTLE MISTAKES HER HUSBAND
FOR A HIGHWAYMAN.
(Illustration by C. Morten—1800's)

Sir Charles. *Here, behind this screen.*

Hardcastle. *Aye, aye, make no noise. I'll engage my Kate covers him with confusion at last.*

Marlow. *By heavens, madam, fortune was ever my smallest consideration. Your beauty at first caught my eye; for who could see that without emotion?* (p. 114B)

DECORATIVE SCREEN—ENGLAND—1700's

Marlow. *Joy, my dear George, I give you joy, sincerely. And could I prevail upon my little tyrant here to be less arbitrary, I should be the happiest man alive, if you would return me the favor.*

Hastings (to Miss Hardcastle). *Come, madam, . . . I know you like him, I'm sure he loves you, and you must and shall have him. (p. 119B)*

HAPPY COUPLES JOINED BY LOVE

CRITICAL EXCERPTS

Selected from the many articles, biographies, and critical essays written about Oliver Goldsmith, here are some excerpts that should prove challenging to you. We have included page references to *She Stoops to Conquer,* indicated in parentheses, so that you can review sample passages to help you decide whether to accept or reject the quoted comments.

The first estimate is a quick, overall view of the play by one of Goldsmith's contemporaries. It covers aspects of the play which some eighteenth-century critics considered objectionable: its lack of a moral, its farcical nature, the absence of wit, and the playwright's concept of humor and character.

1. *Dr. Goldsmith has written a comedy—no, it is the lowest of all farces. It is not the subject I condemn, though very vulgar, but the execution. The drift tends to no moral, no edification of any kind. The situations, however, are well imagined, and make one laugh in spite of the grossness of the dialogue, the forced witticisms, and total improbability of the whole plan and conduct. But what disgusts me most is, that though the characters are very low, and aim at low humor, not one of them says a sentence that is natural or marks any character at all.*

> *Letters,* Written by Horace Walpole, May 27 to Rev. William Mason, Cunningham, Editor, Vol. V, 1773.

Much of the same general criticism appeared in a letter to the editor of the *London Packet,* a periodical of the day. It was an anonymous attack on Goldsmith and was signed

"Tom Tickle." (The personal abuse in the last sentence hurt Goldsmith most.)

2. *We are made to laugh at stale, dull jokes, wherein we mistake pleasantry for wit, and grimace for humor; wherein every scene is unnatural and inconsistent with the rules, the laws of nature and of the drama . . . Mr. Goldsmith, correct your arrogance, reduce your vanity, and endeavor to believe, as a man, you are of the plainest sort,—and as an author, but a mortal piece of mediocrity.*

> As quoted by Washington Irving in *Oliver Goldsmith*, Willis Boughton, Editor, Houghton Mifflin Co., 1903.

Concerning the play's farcical nature, classicist Samuel Johnson, the respected dean of a group of leading authors, indicated that he cared little about the fact that Goldsmith used farce in the play and said, "I know of no comedy for many years that has so much exhilarated an audience; that has answered so much the great end of comedy, making an audience merry." Oliver Goldsmith himself, when censured for the play, asked his critic, "Did it make you laugh?" The critic admitted that it had. Goldsmith rested his case and said, "Then that is all I require."

When dissenters complained about the improbability or farcical nature of the plot, such as the episode in which Tony pretends that the coach is on Crackskull Common, about forty miles from home (p. 109T), a later critic observed:

3. *That delightful comedy,* She Stoops to Conquer, *would indeed deserve a volume, and is the best specimen of what an English comedy should be. It illustrates excellently what has been said as to the necessity of the plot depending on the characters, rather than the characters depending on the plot, as the fashion is at present. . . . What a play! We never tire of it. How rich in situations, each the substance of a whole*

play! At the very first sentence the stream of humour begins to flow.

> *Principles of Comedy and Dramatic Effort*, Perry Fitzgerald, 1870.

Fitzgerald suggests two things: first, character determines plot. Even the hostile critic, "Tom Tickle," had said that Tony Lumpkin is not a fool but the most sensible being of the piece. Second, notice that Fitzgerald does approve of the situations in the play. So, too, does a more modern critic who also comments indirectly on "edification":

4. *His great gift for the comedy of character and situation enabled him to achieve in his two plays,* The Good-Natured Man *and* She Stoops to Conquer, *a sort of pure and mirthful comedy—uncomplicated by ethical or social criticism and unspoiled by the fashionable sentimentality of the moment —that is unique in the century.*

> *The Norton Anthology of English Literature*, Vol. I, M. H. Abrams, Editor, W. W. Norton & Co., Inc., 1962.

Both Tony and his mother, Mrs. Hardcastle, regarded as innovations in character by many eighteenth-century theatergoers, supplied the comedy of character mentioned by the previous critic.

Again, concerning farce, a recent writer said:

5. *One forgets that the plot is littered with absurd coincidences and improbabilities because the farcical scenes and vigorous characterizations are all so full of juicy vitality. The booby Tony Lumpkin and his ever-indulgent mother start by amusing and end by engaging us.*

> "Speaking of Books: Oliver Goldsmith," Robert Halsband, *The New York Times Book Review*, October 30, 1966.

Another critic talks of Goldsmith's plot:

6. *The dialogue is seldom witty, but it is lively. . . . But it is the plot, above all, that determines the effectiveness of the play—and the sustained dramatic irony that determines the effectiveness of the plot. Goldsmith had contrived (or perhaps sometimes borrowed) a series of ideal dramatic situations and he developed them naturally without trying to improve the morals of his audience. . . . In* She Stoops to Conquer *he made a complete break. This play often borders on sheer farce; yet its appeal is irresistible, and it can still amuse audiences of all ages and all degrees of sophistication.*

> *Oliver Goldsmith,* Ralph M. Wardle, University of Kansas Press, 1959.

Goldsmith tried to avoid the older sentimental comedy, yet occasionally he did employ the wit or sentiment that older audiences admired. Take, for example, his last lines in the play (p. 120T): ". . . and as you have been mistaken in the mistress, my wish is, that you may never be mistaken in the wife."

Here is another opinion concerning "sentiment":

7. *Whatever its absurdities, the action seems to move naturally and among natural, homely people—not the artificially sensitive persons found in sentimental comedy nor the hard, brittle wits of high comedy. The characters are all easily individualized—drawn again in the "humorous" Jonsonian fashion—and they are all individuals new to the drama of their day. The historic excellence of the work lies not in the fact that it is apparently anti-sentimental or that it is obviously attempting a revival of the comedy of manners. It is* sui generis, *not sentimental and not overly anti-sentimental. It has been likened to the work of Farquhar, but it is better written and is morally innocent. . . . The play has succeeded*

perfectly in being what its author hoped it would be—one of the most entertaining plays in England.

> A Literary History of England, Alfred C. Baugh, Editor, Appleton-Century-Crofts, Inc., 1948.

Notice that in the next commentary the critic *does* find sparkling wit in *She Stoops to Conquer:*

8. *He at least lived long enough to witness the brilliant beginning of a dramatic triumph which has lasted till our day, and which only one other comedy written since,* The School for Scandal, *can be said to have rivaled. Macaulay calls it "an incomparable farce in five acts," its rollicking drollery and sparkling wit are fitting to amuse all generations, and its dramatic skill is a victory of true inventive genius.*

> "Oliver Goldsmith," George M. Towle, *Appleton's Journal*, Vol. 11, 1874.

Moreover, Dickinson, whose comments follow, discusses Goldsmith's adherence to his principles of the drama in contrast to the principles of other playwrights:

9. *The merits of Goldsmith as a playwright lie close to the surface, and are easily discernible by a sympathetic reader. They are made more manifest when one studies, as we have done, the conditions under which the average drama of his day was written. In the larger matters of structure and design, hardly an adverse criticism can be made of these plays. The development of the story is steady, unforced, and transparent from the beginning to the end . . . . But within the limits of the plays, Goldsmith was rigorously consistent with his . . . principles. His art of the stage was something more than a return from stage types to nature; it depended upon an exaggeration of nature for the purposes of the ludicrous . . .* She Stoops to Conquer, *more lusty with forces of*

laughter, effectively demolished the old comedy, and assumed an abiding place on the English stage.

The Plays of Oliver Goldsmith,
Thomas H. Dickinson, Houghton
Mifflin Co., 1908.

Perhaps the traditionalists of the eighteenth century were annoyed with Goldsmith's mild break with the classical principles of the drama—the unities of time, place, and action. The place and action of *She Stoops to Conquer* shifts from the chamber in Hardcastle's country mansion (p. 7T) to the alehouse room (p. 16T) and elsewhere, and the time unity is not strictly observed. If the violation of these unities is of importance to you, then you may want to quarrel with the structure of the play. How closely do modern dramatists adhere to these principles?

Lest you get the impression that Goldsmith's contemporaries were too severe with him, here is a review by a spectator after the opening performance of the play:

10. *The Comedy is written by Dr. Goldsmith and is founded on a plot exceedingly probable and fertile; each Act contains a great deal of natural business and incident; the characters are for the most part entirely original; they are well drawn, highly finished, and admirably supported from the first to the last scene of the piece. It abounds with genuine wit, and humor, . . . forced witticisms, or absurd conceits; the audience are kept in a continual roar; occasionally a sentiment is delivered, but then it arises naturally from the fable and the character. The dialogue is nervous and spirited; no attempt is made by the author to avail himself of the vitiated taste of the times; he has offered the public a true comic picture which pleased though it differed essentially in manner, skill and finishing from those which of late years have been received and encouraged.*

As quoted by Stephen Gwynn in
Oliver Goldsmith, T. Butterworth,
1935.

The following two statements may give you a more balanced opinion of this playwright:

11. *For accurate research or grave disquisition, he* [Goldsmith] *was not well qualified by nature or by education. He knew nothing accurately; his reading had been desultory; nor had he meditated deeply on what he had read. He had seen much of the world; but he had noticed and retained little more of what he had seen than some grotesque incidents and characters which happen to strike his fancy. But, though his mind was very scantily stored with materials, he used what materials he had in such a way as to produce a wonderful effect. There have been many greater writers; but perhaps no writer was ever more uniformly agreeable.*

> Oliver Goldsmith, Critical and Historical Essays, Thomas Babington Macaulay, 1843.

12. *Goldsmith was not erudite. He was not strikingly original. He was not mystically imaginative. He offered no creed to interpret life. He was content with common sense, common humanity, gaiety and grace. Yet his pen had some touch that dozens of his fellow hacks had not . . . I cannot call* She Stoops to Conquer *one of the world's great plays; nor rank Goldsmith as playwright with his countrymen Sheridan, Shaw, Wilde, or Synge.*

> The Search for Good Sense: Four Eighteenth-Century Characters, F. L. Lucas, Cassell & Co., Ltd., 1958.

Oliver Goldsmith did not claim to be an innovator, and as Wardle once said, "He was not a profound thinker; he did not change men's minds." Critics agree in general that Goldsmith was a capable writer whose epitaph included these words by Johnson: "He left scarce any style of writing untouched, and touched nothing that he did not adorn." In making your final judgment of the play, consider the reasons why it has retained lasting appeal both in the classroom, where it is so often studied, and on the stage, where it is frequently revived. Indeed, what characteristics do most of us have that make us chuckle at the improbabilities of a farce, even when serious critics condemn it for defying logic and nature?

ACT III

Enter Hardcastle *solus.*

HARDCASTLE. What could my old friend Sir Charles mean by recommending his son as the modestest young man in town? To me he appears the most impudent piece of brass that ever spoke with a tongue. He has taken possession of the easy chair by the fireside already. He took off his boots in the parlor, and desired me to see them taken care of. I'm desirous to know how his impudence affects my daughter. —She will certainly be shocked at it.

Enter Miss Hardcastle, *plainly dressed.*

HARDCASTLE. Well, my Kate, I see you have changed your dress, as I bid you; and yet, I believe, there was no great occasion.

MISS HARDCASTLE. I find such a pleasure, sir, in obeying your commands, that I take care to observe them without ever debating their propriety.

HARDCASTLE. And yet, Kate, I sometimes give you

some cause, particularly when I recommended my *modest* gentleman to you as a lover today.

MISS HARDCASTLE. You taught me to expect something extraordinary, and I find the original exceeds the description!

HARDCASTLE. I was never so surprised in my life! He has quite confounded all my faculties!

MISS HARDCASTLE. I never saw anything like it: and a man of the world, too!

HARDCASTLE. Aye, he learned it all abroad—what a fool was I, to think a young man could learn modesty by traveling. He might as soon learn wit at a masquerade.

MISS HARDCASTLE. It seems all natural to him.

HARDCASTLE. A good deal assisted by bad company and a French dancing master.

MISS HARDCASTLE. Sure, you mistake papa! A French dancing master could never have taught him that timid look—that awkward address—that bashful manner—

HARDCASTLE. Whose look? whose manner, child?

MISS HARDCASTLE. Mr. Marlow's: his **mauvaise honte,** his timidity, struck me at the first sight.

HARDCASTLE. Then your first sight deceived you; for I think him one of the most brazen first sights that ever astonished my senses!

MISS HARDCASTLE. Sure, sir, you **rally!** I never saw anyone so modest.

---

mauvaise honte: literally, "bad or wrong shame" in French (maw vez ohnt), translatable as "false shame" or "shyness"

rally: ridicule or "kid"

HARDCASTLE. And can you be serious! I never saw such a bouncing, swaggering puppy since I was born. Bully Dawson was but a fool to him.

MISS HARDCASTLE. Surprising! He met me with a respectful bow, a stammering voice, and a look fixed on the ground.

HARDCASTLE. He met me with a loud voice, a lordly air, and a familiarity that made my blood freeze again.

MISS HARDCASTLE. He treated me with diffidence and respect; censured the manners of the age; admired the prudence of girls that never laughed; tired me with apologies for being tiresome; then left the room with a bow, and "Madam, I would not for the world detain you."

HARDCASTLE. He spoke to me as if he knew me all his life before; asked twenty questions, and never waited for an answer; interrupted my best remarks with some silly pun; and when I was in my best story of the Duke of Marlborough and Prince Eugene, he asked if I had not a good hand at making punch. Yes, Kate, he asked your father if he was a maker of punch!

MISS HARDCASTLE. One of us must certainly be mistaken.

HARDCASTLE. If he be what he has shown himself, I'm determined he shall never have my consent.

MISS HARDCASTLE. And if he be the sullen thing I take him, he shall never have mine.

Bully Dawson: a notorious early eighteenth-century scoundrel

HARDCASTLE. In one thing then we are agreed—
to reject him.

MISS HARDCASTLE. Yes: but upon conditions. For
if you should find him less impudent, and I more
presuming; if you find him more respectful, and I
more **importunate**—I don't know—the fellow is well
enough for a man. Certainly we don't meet many
such at a horse race in the country.

HARDCASTLE. If we should find him so—but that's
impossible. The first appearance has done my business. I'm seldom deceived in that.

MISS HARDCASTLE. And yet there may be many
good qualities under that first appearance.

HARDCASTLE. Aye, when a girl finds a fellow's outside to her taste, she then sets about guessing the
rest of his furniture. With her, a smooth face stands
for good sense, and a genteel figure for every virtue.

MISS HARDCASTLE. I hope, sir, a conversation be-
gun with a compliment to my good sense won't end
with a sneer at my understanding?

HARDCASTLE. Pardon me, Kate. But if young Mr.
Brazen can find the art of reconciling contradictions,
he may please us both, perhaps.

MISS HARDCASTLE. And as one of us must be
mistaken, what if we go to make further discoveries?

HARDCASTLE. Agreed. But depend on't I'm in the
right.

MISS HARDCASTLE. And depend on't I'm not much
in the wrong. *Exeunt.*

---

importunate: pleading, beseeching

Enter Tony, *running in with a casket.*

TONY. Ecod! I have got them. Here they are. My cousin Con's necklaces, **bobs** and all. My mother shan't cheat the poor souls out of their fortin neither. Oh! my genius, is that you?

Enter Hastings.

HASTINGS. My dear friend, how have you managed with your mother? I hope you have amused her with pretending love for your cousin, and that you are willing to be reconciled at last? Our horses will be refreshed in a short time, and we shall soon be ready to set off.

TONY. And here's something to bear your charges by the way. (*Giving the casket.*) Your sweetheart's jewels. Keep them, and hang those, I say, that would rob you of one of them.

HASTINGS. But how have you procured them from your mother?

TONY. Ask me no questions, and I'll tell you no fibs. I procured them by the rule of thumb. If I had not a key to every drawer in mother's bureau, how could I go to the alehouse so often as I do? An honest man may rob himself of his own at any time.

HASTINGS. Thousands do it every day. But to be plain with you, Miss Neville is endeavoring to pro-

---

bobs: dangling jewelry like pendants

cure them from her aunt this very instant. If she succeeds, it will be the most delicate way at least of obtaining them.

Tony. Well, keep them, till you know how it will be. But I know how it will be well enough; she'd as soon part with the only sound tooth in her head!

Hastings. But I dread the effects of her resentment, when she finds she has lost them.

Tony. Never you mind her resentment, leave *me* to manage that. I don't value her resentment the bounce of a **cracker**. Zounds! here they are! **Morrice!** prance!

Exit Hastings.

Tony, Mrs. Hardcastle, *and* Miss Neville.

Mrs. Hardcastle. Indeed, Constance, you amaze me. Such a girl as you want jewels? It will be time enough for jewels, my dear, twenty years hence, when your beauty begins to want repairs.

Miss Neville. But what will repair beauty at forty, will certainly improve it at twenty, madam.

Mrs. Hardcastle. Yours, my dear, can admit of none. That natural blush is beyond a thousand ornaments. Besides, child, jewels are quite out at present. Don't you see half the ladies of our acquaintance, my Lady Kill-daylight, and Mrs. Crump, and the rest of them, carry their jewels to town,

---

cracker: noise of an exploding firecracker

Morrice: "Get going." Morrice is another spelling for Morris dance; a slang command to start such a country dance.

and bring nothing but paste and **marcasites** back?

MISS NEVILLE. But who knows, madam, but somebody that shall be nameless would like me best with all my little finery about me?

MRS. HARDCASTLE. Consult your glass, my dear, and then see, if with such a pair of eyes, you want any better sparklers. What do you think, Tony, my dear, does your cousin Con want any jewels, in your eyes, to set off her beauty?

TONY. That's as thereafter may be.

MISS NEVILLE. My dear aunt, if you knew how it would oblige me.

MRS. HARDCASTLE. A parcel of old-fashioned rose and **table-cut things.** They would make you look like the court of King Solomon at a puppet show. Besides, I believe I can't readily come at them. They may be missing, for aught I know to the contrary.

TONY (*apart to* Mrs. Hardcastle). Then why don't you tell her so at once, as she's so longing for them. Tell her they're lost. It's the only way to quiet her. Say they're lost, and call me to bear witness.

MRS. HARDCASTLE (*apart to* Tony). You know, my dear, I'm only keeping them for you. So if I say they're gone, you'll bear me witness, will you? He! he! he!

TONY. Never fear me. Ecod! I'll say I saw them taken out with my own eyes.

MISS NEVILLE. I desire them but for a day, madam.

---

marcasites: crystallized forms of iron pyrites (fool's gold) used as costume jewelry in the eighteenth century

table-cut things: inexpensive gems not custom-cut with many facets

Just to be permitted to show them as relics, and then they may be locked up again.

MRS. HARDCASTLE. To be plain with you, my dear Constance, if I could find them, you should have them. They're missing, I assure you. Lost, for aught I know; but we must have patience wherever they are.

MISS NEVILLE. I'll not believe it; this is but a shallow pretense to deny me. I know they're too valuable to be so slightly kept, and as you are to answer for the loss—

MRS. HARDCASTLE. Don't be alarmed, Constance. If they be lost, I must restore an equivalent. But my son knows they are missing, and not to be found.

TONY. That I can bear witness to. They are missing, and not to be found, I'll take my oath on't.

MRS. HARDCASTLE. You must learn resignation, my dear; for though we lose our fortune, yet we should not lose our patience. See me, how calm I am.

MISS NEVILLE. Aye, people are generally calm at the misfortunes of others.

MRS. HARDCASTLE. Now, I wonder a girl of your good sense should waste a thought upon such *trumpery*. We shall soon find them; and, in the meantime, you shall make use of my garnets till your jewels be found.

MISS NEVILLE. I detest garnets.

MRS. HARDCASTLE. The most becoming things in the world to set off a clear complexion. You have often seen how well they look upon me. You *shall* have them.   *Exit.*

Miss Neville. I dislike them of all things. You shan't stir. Was ever anything so provoking to mislay my own jewels, and force me to wear her trumpery.

Tony. Don't be a fool. If she gives you the garnets, take what you can get. The jewels are your own already. I have stolen them out of her bureau, and she does not know it. Fly to your **spark,** he'll tell you more of the matter. Leave me to manage *her.*

Miss Neville. My dear cousin!

Tony. Vanish. She's here, and has missed them already. [*Exit* Miss Neville.] Zounds! how she fidgets and spits about like a **catherine wheel!**

Enter Mrs. Hardcastle.

Mrs. Hardcastle. Confusion! thieves! robbers! We are cheated, plundered, broke open, undone!

Tony. What's the matter, what's the matter, mamma? I hope nothing has happened to any of the good family!

Mrs. Hardcastle. We are robbed. My bureau has been broke open, the jewels taken out, and I'm undone!

Tony. Oh! is that all! Ha! ha! ha! By the laws,

---

spark: sweetheart
catherine wheel: a pinwheel firecracker which throws off sparks as it revolves

I never saw it better acted in my life. Ecod, I thought
you was ruined in earnest, ha, ha, ha!

MRS. HARDCASTLE. Why, boy, I *am* ruined in
earnest. My bureau has been broke open, and all
taken away.

TONY. Stick to that; ha, ha, ha! stick to that. I'll
bear witness, you know, call me to bear witness.

MRS. HARDCASTLE. I tell you, Tony, by all that's
precious, the jewels are gone, and I shall be ruined
forever.

TONY. Sure I know they're gone, and I am to say
so.

MRS. HARDCASTLE. My dearest Tony, but hear me.
They're gone, I say.

TONY. By the laws, mamma, you make me for to
laugh, ha! ha! I know who took them well enough,
ha! ha! ha!

MRS. HARDCASTLE. Was there ever such a blockhead, that can't tell the difference between jest and
earnest? I tell you I'm not in jest, booby!

TONY. That's right, that's right! You must be in
a bitter passion, and then nobody will suspect either
of us. I'll bear witness that they are gone.

MRS. HARDCASTLE. Was there ever such a cross-
grained brute, that won't hear me? Can you bear
witness that you're no better than a fool? Was ever
poor woman so beset with fools on one hand, and
thieves on the other?

TONY. I can bear witness to that.

MRS. HARDCASTLE. Bear witness again, you blockhead you, and I'll turn you out of the room directly.
My poor niece, what will become of *her?* Do you

laugh, you unfeeling brute, as if you enjoyed my distress?

TONY. I can bear witness to that.

MRS. HARDCASTLE. Do you insult me, monster? I'll teach you to vex your mother, I will.

TONY. I can bear witness to that. (*He runs off, she follows him.*)

Enter Miss Hardcastle *and* Maid.

MISS HARDCASTLE. What an unaccountable creature is that brother of mine, to send them to the house as an inn, ha! ha! I don't wonder at his impudence.

MAID. But what is more, madam, the young gentleman as you passed by in your present dress, asked me if you were the barmaid. He mistook you for the barmaid, madam!

MISS HARDCASTLE. Did he? Then as I live I'm resolved to keep up the delusion. Tell me, Pimple, how do you like my present dress? Don't you think I look something like Cherry in **The Beaux' Stratagem?**

MAID. It's the dress, madam, that every lady wears in the country, but when she visits or receives company.

MISS HARDCASTLE. And are you sure he does not remember my face or person?

MAID. Certain of it.

The Beaux' Stratagem: a comedy by George Farquhar produced in 1707. Cherry was a character, the innkeeper's daughter, in the play.

MISS HARDCASTLE. I vow, I thought so; for though we spoke for some time together, yet his fears were such, that he never once looked up during the interview. Indeed, if he had, my bonnet would have kept him from seeing me.

MAID. But what do you hope from keeping him in his mistake?

MISS HARDCASTLE. In the first place, I shall be *seen*, and that is no small advantage to a girl who brings her face to market. Then I shall perhaps make an acquaintance, and that's no small victory gained over one who never addresses any but the wildest of her sex. But my chief aim is to take my gentleman off his guard, and like an invisible champion of romance, examine the giant's force before I offer to combat.

MAID. But you are sure you can act your part, and disguise your voice, so that he may mistake that, as he has already mistaken your person?

MISS HARDCASTLE. Never fear me. I think I have got the true **bar cant.** Did your honor call?—Attend the **Lion** there. —Pipes and tobacco for the **Angel.** —The **Lamb** has been outrageous this half hour.

MAID. It will do, madam. But he's here.

Exit Maid.

---

    bar cant: the slang used by bartenders
    Lion, Angel, Lamb: names, instead of numbers, for rooms in an inn. In this case, of course, Kate is making up names for the pretended inn.

Enter Marlow.

MARLOW. What a bawling in every part of the house; I have scarce a moment's repose. If I go to the best room, there I find my host and his story. If I fly to the gallery, there we have my hostess with her curtsy down to the ground. I have at last got a moment to myself, and now for recollection. *(Walks and muses.)*

MISS HARDCASTLE. Did you call, sir? Did your honor call?

MARLOW *(musing).* As for Miss Hardcastle, she's too grave and sentimental for me.

MISS HARDCASTLE. Did your honor call? *(She still places herself before him, he turning away.)*

MARLOW. No, child. *(Musing.)* Besides from the glimpse I had of her, I think she squints.

MISS HARDCASTLE. I'm sure, sir, I heard the bell ring.

MARLOW. No, no. *(Musing.)* I have pleased my father, however, by coming down, and I'll tomorrow please myself by returning. *(Taking out his* **tablets,** *and perusing.)*

MISS HARDCASTLE. Perhaps the other gentleman called, sir?

MARLOW. I tell you, no.

MISS HARDCASTLE. I should be glad to know, sir. We have such a parcel of servants.

MARLOW. No, no, I tell you. *(Looks full in her*

---

tablets: memo books

face.) Yes, child, I think I did call. I wanted—I wanted—I vow, child, you are vastly handsome.

MISS HARDCASTLE. O la, sir, you'll make one ashamed.

MARLOW. Never saw a more sprightly, malicious eye. Yes, yes, my dear, I did call. Have you got any of your—a—what d'ye call it in the house?

MISS HARDCASTLE. No, sir, we have been out of that these ten days.

MARLOW. One may call in this house, I find, to very little purpose. Suppose I should call for a taste, just by way of trial, of the **nectar** of your lips; perhaps I might be disappointed in that, too.

MISS HARDCASTLE. Nectar! nectar! that's a liquor there's no call for in these parts. French, I suppose. We keep no French wines here, sir.

MARLOW. Of true English growth, I assure you.

MISS HARDCASTLE. Then it's odd I should not know it. We brew all sorts of wines in this house, and I have lived here these eighteen years.

MARLOW. Eighteen years! Why one would think, child, you kept the bar before you were born. How old are you?

MISS HARDCASTLE. O! sir, I must not tell my age. They say women and music should never be dated.

MARLOW. To guess at this distance, you can't be much above forty. (*Approaching.*) Yet nearer I don't think so much. (*Approaching.*) By coming close to some women they look younger still; but when

---

nectar: the special drink of the classical gods

we come very close indeed— *(Attempting to kiss her.)*

Miss Hardcastle. Pray, sir, keep your distance. One would think you wanted to know one's age as they do horses, by mark of mouth.

Marlow. I protest, child, you use me extremely ill. If you keep me at this distance, how is it possible you and I can be ever acquainted?

Miss Hardcastle. And who wants to be acquainted with you? I want no such acquaintance, not I. I'm sure you did not treat Miss Hardcastle that was here awhile ago in this **obstropalous** manner. I'll warrant me, before her you looked dashed, and kept bowing to the ground, and talked, for all the world, as if you was before a justice of peace.

Marlow *(aside)*. Egad! she has hit it, sure enough. *(To her.)* In awe of her, child? Ha! ha! ha! A mere awkward, squinting thing! No, no! I find you don't know me. I laughed, and rallied her a little; but I was unwilling to be too severe. No, I could not be too severe, curse me!

Miss Hardcastle. Oh! then, sir, you are a favorite, I find, among the ladies?

Marlow. Yes, my dear, a great favorite. And yet, hang me, I don't see what they find in me to follow. At the Ladies' Club in town I'm called their agreeable Rattle. Rattle, child, is not my real name, but one I'm known by. My name is Solomons. Mr. Solo-

---

obstropalous: Kate is imitating an uneducated barmaid clumsily trying to use big words such as "obstreperous."

mons, my dear, at your service. (*Offering to salute her.*)

MISS HARDCASTLE. Hold, sir; you are introducing me to your club, not to yourself. And you're so great a favorite there, you say?

MARLOW. Yes, my dear. There's Mrs. Mantrap, Lady Betty Blackleg, the Countess of Sligo, Mrs. Langhorns, old Miss Biddy Buckskin and your humble servant, keep up the spirit of the place.

MISS HARDCASTLE. Then it's a very merry place, I suppose?

MARLOW. Yes, as merry as cards, suppers, wine, and old women can make us.

MISS HARDCASTLE. And their agreeable Rattle, ha! ha! ha!

MARLOW (*aside*). Egad! I don't quite like this chit. She looks knowing, methinks. You laugh, child!

MISS HARDCASTLE. I can't but laugh to think what time they all have for minding their work or their family.

MARLOW (*aside*). All's well, she don't laugh at me. (*To her.*) Do you ever work, child?

MISS HARDCASTLE. Aye, sure. There's not a screen or a quilt in the whole house but what can bear witness to that.

MARLOW. Odso! Then you must show me your embroidery. I embroider and draw patterns myself a little. If you want a judge of your work you must apply to me. (*Seizing her hand.*)

Enter Hardcastle, *who stands in surprise.*

MISS HARDCASTLE. Aye, but the colors don't look well by candlelight. You shall see all in the morning. *(Struggling.)*

MARLOW. And why not now, my angel? Such beauty fires beyond the power of resistance. —Pshaw! the father here! My old luck: I never nicked **seven** that I did not throw **ames-ace** three times following. *Exit* Marlow.

HARDCASTLE. So, madam. So I find *this* is your *modest* lover. This is your humble admirer that kept his eyes fixed on the ground, and only adored at humble distance. Kate, Kate, art thou not ashamed to deceive your father so?

MISS HARDCASTLE. Never trust me, dear papa, but he's still the modest man I first took him for, you'll be convinced of it as well as I.

HARDCASTLE. By the hand of my body, I believe his impudence is infectious! Didn't I see him seize your hand? Didn't I see him haul you about like a milkmaid? And now you talk of his respect and his modesty, forsooth!

MISS HARDCASTLE. But if I shortly convince you of his modesty that he has only the faults that will

---

Seven, ames-ace: dice-shooting terms. The number seven on a first throw is a winning number, but Marlow says that his luck as a dice-shooter is usually so bad that when he does shoot a seven, his next three throws are always "ambs" or "ames-ace" (double "ones"), losing numbers.

pass off with time, and the virtues that will improve with age, I hope you'll forgive him.

HARDCASTLE. The girl would actually make one run mad! I tell you I'll not be convinced. I am convinced. He has scarcely been three hours in the house, and he has already encroached on all my prerogatives. You may like his impudence, and call it modesty. But my son-in-law, madam, must have very different qualifications.

MISS HARDCASTLE. Sir, I ask but this night to convince you.

HARDCASTLE. You shall not have half the time, for I have thoughts of turning him out this very hour.

MISS HARDCASTLE. Give me that hour then, and I hope to satisfy you.

HARDCASTLE. Well, an hour let it be then. But I'll have no trifling with your father. All fair and open, do you mind me?

MISS HARDCASTLE. I hope, sir, you have ever found that I considered your commands as my pride; for your kindness is such, that my duty as yet has been inclination.

SHE STOOPS
TO
CONQUER

— •• —

ACT IV

ACT IV

Enter Hastings *and* Miss Neville.

HASTINGS. You surprise me! Sir Charles Marlow expected here this night! Where have you had your information?

MISS NEVILLE. You may depend upon it. I just saw his letter to Mr. Hardcastle, in which he tells him he intends setting out a few hours after his son.

HASTINGS. Then, my Constance, all must be completed before he arrives. He knows me; and should he find me here, would discover my name, and perhaps my designs, to the rest of the family.

MISS NEVILLE. The jewels, I hope, are safe?

HASTINGS. Yes, yes. I have sent them to Marlow, who keeps the keys of our baggage. In the meantime, I'll go to prepare matters for our elopement. I have had the squire's promise of a fresh pair of horses; and, if I should not see him again, will write him further directions. *Exit.*

MISS NEVILLE. Well! success attend you. In the meantime, I'll go amuse my aunt with the old pretense of a violent passion for my cousin. *Exit.*

Enter Marlow, *followed by* Servant.

MARLOW. I wonder what Hastings could mean by sending me so valuable a thing as a casket to keep for him, when he knows the only place I have is the seat of a post coach at an inn door. Have you deposited the casket with the landlady, as I ordered you? Have you put it into her own hands?

SERVANT. Yes, your honor.

MARLOW. She said she'd keep it safe, did she?

SERVANT. Yes, she said she'd keep it safe enough; she asked me how I came by it, and she said she had a great mind to make me give an account of myself.   *Exit* Servant.

MARLOW. Ha! ha! ha! They're safe, however. What an unaccountable set of beings have we got amongst! This little barmaid, though, runs in my head most strangely, and drives out the absurdities of all the rest of the family. She's mine, she must be mine, or I'm greatly mistaken.

Enter Hastings.

HASTINGS. Bless me! I quite forgot to tell her that I intended to prepare at the bottom of the garden. Marlow here, and in spirits too!

MARLOW. Give me joy, George! Crown me, shadow me with laurels! Well, George, after all, we modest fellows don't want for success among the women.

HASTINGS. Some women, you mean. But what success has your honor's modesty been crowned with now, that it grows so insolent upon us?

MARLOW. Didn't you see the tempting, brisk, lovely little thing that runs about the house with a bunch of keys to its girdle?

HASTINGS. Well! and what then?

MARLOW. She's mine, you rogue you. Such fire, such motions, such eyes, such lips—but, egad! she would not let me kiss them though.

HASTINGS. But are you so sure, so very sure of her?

MARLOW. Why man, she talked of showing me her work above stairs and I am to improve the pattern.

HASTINGS. But how can *you*, Charles, go about to rob a woman of her honor?

MARLOW. Pshaw! pshaw! We all know the honor of a barmaid of an inn. I don't intend to *rob* her, take my word for it; there's nothing in this house I shan't honestly *pay* for.

HASTINGS. I believe the girl has virtue.

MARLOW. And if she has, I should be the last man in the world that would attempt to corrupt it.

HASTINGS. You have taken care, I hope, of the casket I sent you to lock up? It's in safety?

MARLOW. Yes, yes. It's safe enough. I have taken care of it. But how could you think the seat of a post coach at an inn door a place of safety? Ah! numskull! I have taken better precautions for you than you did for yourself. I have—

HASTINGS. What?

MARLOW. I have sent it to the landlady to keep for you.

HASTINGS. To the landlady!

MARLOW. The landlady.

HASTINGS. You did?

MARLOW. I did. She's to be answerable for its forthcoming, you know.

HASTINGS. Yes, she'll bring it forth with a witness.

MARLOW. Wasn't I right? I believe you'll allow that I acted prudently upon this occasion?

HASTINGS (*aside*). He must not see my uneasiness.

MARLOW. You seem a little disconcerted, though, methinks. Sure nothing has happened?

HASTINGS. No, nothing. Never was in better spirits in all my life. And so you left it with the landlady, who, no doubt, very readily undertook the charge?

MARLOW. Rather too readily. For she not only kept the casket, but, through her great precaution, was going to keep the messenger too. Ha! ha! ha!

HASTINGS. He! he! he! They're safe, however.

MARLOW. As a guinea in a miser's purse.

HASTINGS (*aside*). So now all hopes of fortune are at an end, and we must set off without it. (*To him.*) Well, Charles, I'll leave you to your meditations on the pretty barmaid, and, he! he! he! may you be as successful for yourself as you have been for me.

Exit.

MARLOW. Thank ye, George! I ask no more. Ha! ha! ha!

Enter Hardcastle.

HARDCASTLE. I no longer know my own house. It's turned all topsy-turvy. His servants have got drunk already. I'll bear it no longer, and yet, from my respect for his father, I'll be calm. *(To him.)* Mr. Marlow, your servant. I'm your very humble servant. *(Bowing low.)*

MARLOW. Sir, your humble servant. *(Aside.)* What's to be the wonder now?

HARDCASTLE. I believe, sir, you must be sensible, sir, that no man alive ought to be more welcome than your father's son, sir. I hope you think so?

MARLOW. I do, from my soul, sir. I don't want much entreaty. I generally make my father's son welcome wherever he goes.

HARDCASTLE. I believe you do, from my soul, sir. But though I say nothing to your own conduct, that of your servants is insufferable. Their manner of drinking is setting a very bad example in this house, I assure you.

MARLOW. I protest, my very good sir, that's no fault of mine. If they don't drink as they ought, *they* are to blame. I ordered them not to spare the cellar. I did, I assure you. *(To the side scene.)* Here, let one of my servants come up. *(To him.)* My positive directions were, that as I did not drink myself, they should make up for my deficiencies below.

HARDCASTLE. Then they had your orders for what they do! I'm satisfied!

MARLOW. They had, I assure you. You shall hear from one of themselves.

Enter Servant, *drunk.*

MARLOW. You, Jeremy! Come forward, sirrah! What were my orders? Were you not told to drink freely, and call for what you thought fit, for the good of the house?

HARDCASTLE *(aside).* I begin to lose my patience.

JEREMY *(staggering forward).* Please your honor, liberty and Fleet Street forever! Though I'm but a servant, I'm as good as another man. I'll drink for no man before supper, sir, dammy! Good liquor will sit upon a good supper, but a good supper will not sit upon—hiccup—upon my conscience, sir.   *Exit.*

MARLOW. You see, my old friend, the fellow is as drunk as he can possibly be. I don't know what you'd have more, unless you'd have the poor devil soused in a beer barrel.

HARDCASTLE. Zounds! He'll drive me distracted if I contain myself any longer. Mr. Marlow, sir; I have submitted to your insolence for more than four hours, and I see no likelihood of its coming to an end. I'm now resolved to be master here, sir, and I desire that you and your drunken pack may leave my house directly.

MARLOW. Leave your house!—Sure, you jest, my

---

liberty and Fleet Street: The slogan is connected with the name of John Wilkes (1727–1797), an English political reformer who was the idol of London mobs. Fleet Street became synonymous with newspapers only at the end of the eighteenth century; at the time of the play, it was well-known for its drinking places.

good friend! What, when I'm doing what I can to please you!

HARDCASTLE. I tell you, sir, you don't please me; so I desire you'll leave my house.

MARLOW. Sure, you cannot be serious! At this time o' night, and such a night! You only mean to banter me!

HARDCASTLE. I tell you, sir, I'm serious; and, now that my passions are roused, I say this house is mine, sir; this house is mine, and I command you to leave it directly.

MARLOW. Ha! ha! ha! A puddle in a storm. I shan't stir a step, I assure you. *(In a serious tone.)* This your house, fellow! It's my house. This is my house. Mine, while I choose to stay. What right have you to bid me leave this house, sir? I never met with such impudence, curse me, never in my whole life before.

HARDCASTLE. Nor I, confound me if ever I did! To come to my house, to call for what he likes, to turn me out of my own chair, to insult the family, to order his servants to get drunk, and then to tell me *This house is mine, sir.* By all that's impudent, it makes me laugh. Ha! ha! ha! Pray sir *(bantering)*, as you take the house, what think you of taking the rest of the furniture? There's a pair of silver candlesticks, and there's a firescreen, and here's a pair of brazen-nosed bellows, perhaps you may take a fancy to them?

MARLOW. Bring me your bill, sir, bring me your bill, and let's make no more words about it.

HARDCASTLE. There are a set of prints, too. What

think you of **"The Rake's Progress"** for your own apartment?

MARLOW. Bring me your bill, I say; and I'll leave you and your infernal house directly.

HARDCASTLE. Then there's a mahogany table, that you may see your own face in.

MARLOW. My bill, I say.

HARDCASTLE. I had forgot the great chair, for your own particular slumbers, after a hearty meal.

MARLOW. Zounds! bring me my bill, I say, and let's hear no more on't.

HARDCASTLE. Young man, young man, from your father's letter to me, I was taught to expect a well-bred modest man as a visitor here, but now I find him no better than a *coxcomb* and a bully; but he will be down here presently, and shall hear more of it. *Exit.*

MARLOW. How's this! Sure I have not mistaken the house! Everything looks like an inn. The servants cry "Coming"; the attendance is awkward; the bar-maid, too, to attend us. But she's here, and will further inform me. Whither so fast, child? A word with you.

Enter Miss Hardcastle.

MISS HARDCASTLE. Let it be short, then. I'm in a hurry. *(Aside.)* I believe he begins to find out his

---

"The Rake's Progress": the series of engravings published in 1735 by William Hogarth (1697–1764), the famous English pictorial satirist, which showed the ruin of a degrading character

mistake. But it's too soon quite to undeceive him.

MARLOW. Pray, child, answer me one question. What are you, and what may your business in this house be?

MISS HARDCASTLE. A relation of the family, sir.

MARLOW. What, a poor relation?

MISS HARDCASTLE. Yes, sir. A poor relation appointed to keep the keys, and to see that the guests want nothing in my power to give them.

MARLOW. That is, you act as the barmaid of this inn.

MISS HARDCASTLE. Inn. O lawl What brought that in your head? One of the best families in the country keep an innl Ha, ha, ha, old Mr. Hardcastle's house an innl

MARLOW. Mr. Hardcastle's housel Is this house Mr. Hardcastle's house, child?

MISS HARDCASTLE. Aye, sure. Whose else should it be?

MARLOW. So then all's out, and I have been damnably imposed on. O, confound my stupid head, I shall be laughed at over the whole town. I shall be stuck up in *caricatura* in all the print shops. "The Dullissimo Maccaroni." To mistake this house of all others for an inn, and my father's old friend for an innkeeper. What a swaggering puppy must he take me for. What a silly puppy do I find

---

"The Dullissimo Maccaroni": Marlow is afraid that his caricature will be posted around town, a custom of the day, as the stupidest or most boring dandy ("macaroni") in London for his actions in mistaking a country home as an inn.

myself. There again, may I be hanged, my dear, but I mistook you for the barmaid.

Miss Hardcastle. Dear me! dear me! I'm sure there's nothing in my **behavour** to put me upon a level with one of that stamp.

Marlow. Nothing, my dear, nothing. But I was in for a list of blunders, and could not help making you a subscriber. My stupidity saw everything the wrong way. I mistook your assiduity for assurance, and your simplicity for allurement. But it's over. This house I no more show my face in!

Miss Hardcastle. I hope, sir, I have done nothing to disoblige you. I'm sure I should be sorry to affront any gentleman who has been so polite, and said so many civil things to me. I'm sure I should be sorry *(pretending to cry)* if he left the family upon my account. I'm sure I should be sorry people said anything amiss, since I have no fortune but my character.

Marlow *(aside)*. By heaven, she weeps. This is the first mark of tenderness I ever had from a modest woman, and it touches me. *(To her.)* Excuse me, my lovely girl, you are the only part of the family I leave with reluctance. But to be plain with you, the difference of our birth, fortune and education, make an honorable connection impossible, and I can never harbor a thought of seducing simplicity that trusted in my honor, or bringing ruin upon one whose only fault was being too lovely.

Miss Hardcastle *(aside)*. Generous man! I now

---

behavour: Kate, again as a barmaid, is purposely mispronouncing her words.

begin to admire him. *(To him.)* But I'm sure my family is as good as Miss Hardcastle's, and though I'm poor, that's no great misfortune to a contented mind, and, until this moment, I never thought that it was bad to want fortune.

MARLOW. And why now, my pretty simplicity?

MISS HARDCASTLE. Because it puts me at a distance from one, that if I had a thousand pounds I would give it all to.

MARLOW *(aside)*. This simplicity bewitches me, so that if I stay I'm undone. I must make one bold effort, and leave her. *(To her.)* Your partiality in my favor, my dear, touches me most sensibly, and were I to live for myself alone, I could easily fix my choice. But I owe too much to the opinion of the world, too much to the authority of a father, so that —I can scarcely speak it—it affects me. Farewell.

Exit.

MISS HARDCASTLE. I never knew half his merit till now. He shall not go, if I have power or art to detain him. I'll still preserve the character in which I stooped to conquer, but will undeceive my papa, who, perhaps, may laugh him out of his resolution.

Exit.

Enter Tony, Miss Neville.

TONY. Aye, you may steal for yourselves the next time. I have done my duty. She has got the jewels again, that's a sure thing; but she believes it was all a mistake of the servants.

MISS NEVILLE. But, my dear cousin, sure, you

won't forsake us in this distress. If she in the least suspects that I am going off, I shall certainly be locked up, or sent to my Aunt Pedigree's which is ten times worse.

TONY. To be sure, aunts of all kinds are damned bad things. But what can I do? I have got you a pair of horses that will fly like **Whistlejacket,** and I'm sure you can't say but I have courted you nicely before her face. Here she comes, we must court a bit or two more, for fear she should suspect us. *(They retire, and seem to fondle.)*

Enter Mrs. Hardcastle.

MRS. HARDCASTLE. Well, I was greatly fluttered, to be sure. But my son tells me it was all a mistake of the servants. I shan't be easy, however, till they are fairly married, and then let her keep her own fortune. But what do I see? Fondling together, as I'm alive! I never saw Tony so sprightly before. Ah! have I caught you, my pretty doves? What, billing, exchanging stolen glances, and broken murmurs! Ah!

TONY. As for murmurs, mother, we grumble a little now and then, to be sure. But there's no love lost between us.

MRS. HARDCASTLE. A mere sprinkling, Tony, upon the flame, only to make it burn brighter.

MISS NEVILLE. Cousin Tony promises to give us more of his company at home. Indeed, he shan't

---

Whistlejacket: the name of a famous racehorse

leave us any more. It won't leave us, cousin Tony, will it?

TONY. O! it's a pretty creature. No, I'd sooner leave my horse in a pound, than leave you when you smile upon one so. Your laugh makes you so becoming.

MISS NEVILLE. Agreeable cousin! Who can help admiring that natural humor, that pleasant, broad, red, thoughtless (*patting his cheek*) ah! it's a bold face.

MRS. HARDCASTLE. Pretty innocence!

TONY. I'm sure I always loved cousin Con's hazel eyes, and her pretty long fingers, that she twists this way and that, over the **haspicholls,** like a parcel of bobbins.

MRS. HARDCASTLE. Ah, he would charm the bird from the tree. I was never so happy before. My boy takes after his father, poor Mr. Lumpkin, exactly. The jewels, my dear Con, shall be yours **incontinently.** You shall have them. Isn't he a sweet boy, my dear? You shall be married tomorrow, and we'll put off the rest of his education, like Dr. Drowsy's sermons, to a fitter opportunity.

Enter Diggory.

DIGGORY. Where's the squire? I have got a letter for your worship.

---

haspicholls: Tony's way of saying harpsichord, the pianolike instrument. He compares the action of Miss Neville's nimble fingers on the keyboard with the action of fingers at work weaving.

incontinently: without reservation or restrictions

TONY. Give it to my mamma. She reads all my letters first.

DIGGORY. I had orders to deliver it into your own hands.

TONY. Who does it come from?

DIGGORY. Your worship mun ask that o' the letter itself.

TONY. I could wish to know, though. (*Turning the letter, and gazing on it.*)   [*Exit* Diggory.]

MISS NEVILLE (*aside*). Undone, undone. A letter to him from Hastings. I know the hand. If my aunt sees it, we are ruined forever. I'll keep her employed a little if I can. (*To Mrs. Hardcastle.*) But I have not told you, madam, of my cousin's smart answer just now to Mr. Marlow. We so laughed. You must know, madam. This way a little, for he must not hear us. (*They confer.*)

TONY (*still gazing*). A damned cramp piece of penmanship, as ever I saw in my life. I can read your print-hand very well. But here there are such handles, and shakes, and dashes, that one can scarce tell the head from the tail. "To Anthony Lumpkin, Esquire." It's very odd, I can read the outside of my letters, where my own name is, well enough. But when I come to open it, it's all—buzz. That's hard, very hard; for the inside of the letter is always the cream of the correspondence.

MRS. HARDCASTLE. Ha! ha! ha! Very well, very well. And so my son was too hard for the philosopher.

MISS NEVILLE. Yes, madam; but you must hear

the rest, madam. A little more this way, or he may hear us. You'll hear how he puzzled him again.

MRS. HARDCASTLE. He seems strangely puzzled now himself, methinks.

TONY (*still gazing*). A damned up-and-down hand, as if it was disguised in liquor. (*Reading.*) "Dear Sir." Aye, that's that. Then there's an *M*, and a *T*, and an *S*, but whether the next be an **"izzard"** or an *R*, confound me, I cannot tell.

MRS. HARDCASTLE. What's that, my dear? Can I give you any assistance?

MISS NEVILLE. Pray, aunt, let me read it. Nobody reads a cramp hand better than I (*twitching the letter from her*). Do you know who it is from?

TONY. Can't tell, except from Dick Ginger the feeder.

MISS NEVILLE. Aye, so it is. (*Pretending to read.*) Dear Squire, Hoping that you're in health, as I am at this present. The gentlemen of the Shakebag club has cut the gentlemen of Goose-green quite out of feather. The odds—um—odd battle—um—long fighting—um, here, here, it's all about cocks, and fighting; it's of no consequence, here, put it up, put it up. (*Thrusting the crumpled letter upon him.*)

TONY. But I tell you, miss, it's of all the consequence in the world. I would not lose the rest of it for a guinea. Here, mother, do you make it out? Of no consequence! (*Giving* Mrs. Hardcastle *the letter.*)

MRS. HARDCASTLE. How's this! (*Reads.*) "Dear

"izzard": the last letter in the alphabet, "Z"

Squire, I'm now waiting for Miss Neville, with a post chaise and pair, at the bottom of the garden but I find my horses yet unable to perform the journey. I expect you'll assist us with a pair of fresh horses, as you promised. Dispatch is necessary, as the hag" —aye, the hag—"your mother, will otherwise suspect us. Yours, Hastings." Grant me patience. I shall run distracted. My rage chokes me.

Miss Neville. I hope, madam, you'll suspend your resentment for a few moments, and not impute to me any impertinence, or sinister design, that belongs to another.

Mrs. Hardcastle (curtsying very low). Fine spoken, madam, you are most miraculously polite and engaging, and quite the very pink of courtesy and circumspection, madam. (Changing her tone.) And you, you great ill-fashioned oaf, with scarce sense enough to keep your mouth shut. Were you, too, joined against me? But I'll defeat all your plots in a moment. As for you, madam, since you have got a pair of fresh horses ready, it would be cruel to disappoint them. So, if you please, instead of running away with your spark, prepare, this very moment, to run off with me. Your old Aunt Pedigree will keep you secure, I'll warrant me. You, too, sir, may mount your horse, and guard us upon the way. Here, Thomas, Roger, Diggory, I'll show you that I wish you better than you do yourselves.   Exit.

Miss Neville. So now I'm completely ruined.

Tony. Aye, that's a sure thing.

Miss Neville. What better could be expected

from being connected with such a stupid fool, and after all the nods and signs I made him.

TONY. By the laws, miss, it was your own cleverness, and not my stupidity, that did your business. You were so nice and so busy with your Shakebags and Goose-greens, that I thought you could never be making believe.

Enter Hastings.

HASTINGS. So, sir, I find by my servant, that you have shown my letter, and betrayed us. Was this well done, young gentleman?

TONY. Here's another. Ask Miss there who betrayed you. Ecod, it was her doing, not mine.

Enter Marlow.

MARLOW. So I have been finely used here among you. Rendered contemptible, driven into ill manners, despised, insulted, laughed at.

TONY. Here's another. We shall have old **Bedlam** broke loose presently.

MISS NEVILLE. And there, sir, is the gentleman to whom we all owe every obligation.

MARLOW. What can I say to him, a mere boy, an idiot, whose ignorance and age are a protection.

Bedlam: popular name for the Hospital of St. Mary of Bethlehem in London, formerly an insane asylum, from which we get the word *bedlam*, meaning "uproar" and "confusion"

HASTINGS. A poor contemptible booby, that would but disgrace correction.

MISS NEVILLE. Yet with cunning and malice enough to make himself merry with all our embarrassments.

HASTINGS. An insensible cub.

MARLOW. Replete with tricks and mischief.

TONY. Bawl damme, but I'll fight you both one after the other—with **baskets**.

MARLOW. As for him, he's below resentment. But your conduct, Mr. Hastings, requires an explanation. You knew of my mistakes, yet would not undeceive me.

HASTINGS. Tortured as I am with my own disappointments, is this a time for explanations? It is not friendly, Mr. Marlow.

MARLOW. But, sir—

MISS NEVILLE. Mr. Marlow, we never kept on your mistake, till it was too late to undeceive you. Be pacified.

Enter Servant.

SERVANT. My mistress desires you'll get ready immediately, madam. The horses are **putting to.** Your hat and things are in the next room. We are to go thirty miles before morning.   *Exit* Servant.

MISS NEVILLE. Well, well; I'll come presently.

MARLOW (*to* Hastings). Was it well done, sir, to

---

baskets: dueling swords with basket-shaped hilts to protect the hands

putting to: being hitched up to the coach

assist in rendering me ridiculous? To hang me out for the scorn of all my acquaintance? Depend upon it, sir, I shall expect an explanation.

HASTINGS. Was it well done, sir, if you're upon that subject, to deliver what I entrusted to yourself, to the care of another, sir?

MISS NEVILLE. Mr. Hastings, Mr. Marlow. Why will you increase my distress by this groundless dispute? I implore, I entreat you—

Enter Servant.

SERVANT. Your cloak, madam. My mistress is impatient.

MISS NEVILLE. I come. [*Exit* Servant.] Pray be pacified. If I leave you thus, I shall die with apprehension!

Enter Servant.

SERVANT. Your fan, muff, and gloves, madam. The horses are waiting. [*Exit* Servant.]

MISS NEVILLE. O, Mr. Marlow! if you knew what a scene of constraint and ill-nature lies before me, I'm sure it would convert your resentment into pity.

MARLOW. I'm so distracted with a variety of passions, that I don't know what I do. Forgive me, madam. George, forgive me. You know my hasty temper, and should not exasperate it.

HASTINGS. The torture of my situation is my only excuse.

MISS NEVILLE. Well, my dear Hastings, if you have that esteem for me that I think, that I am sure you have, your constancy for three years will but increase the happiness of our future connection. If—

MRS. HARDCASTLE (*within*). Miss Neville. Constance, why, Constance, I say!

MISS NEVILLE. I'm coming. Well, constancy. Remember, constancy is the word.   *Exit.*

HASTINGS. My heart! How can I support this? To be so near happiness, and such happiness!

MARLOW (*to* Tony). You see now, young gentleman, the effects of your folly. What might be amusement to you, is here disappointment, and even distress.

TONY (*from a reverie*). Ecod, I have hit it. It's here. Your hands. Yours and yours, my poor Sulky. My boots there, ho! Meet me two hours hence at the **bottom** of the garden; and if you don't find Tony Lumpkin a more good-natur'd fellow than you thought for, I'll give you leave to take my best horse, and Bet Bouncer into the bargain. Come along. My boots, ho!   *Exeunt.*

---

bottom: foot or rear of the garden

SHE STOOPS
TO
CONQUER

ACT V

ACT V

Scene I: Scene continues.

===

Enter Hastings *and* Servant.

HASTINGS. You saw the old lady and Miss Neville drive off, you say?

SERVANT. Yes, your honor. They went off in a post coach, and the young squire went on horseback. They're thirty miles off by this time.

HASTINGS. Then all my hopes are over.

SERVANT. Yes, sir. Old Sir Charles is arrived. He and the old gentleman of the house have been laughing at Mr. Marlow's mistake this half hour. They are coming this way.

HASTINGS. Then I must not be seen. So now to my fruitless appointment at the bottom of the garden. This is about the time. *Exit.*

Enter Sir Charles *and* Hardcastle.

HARDCASTLE. Ha! ha! ha! The peremptory tone in which he sent forth his sublime commands.

SIR CHARLES. And the reserve with which I suppose he treated all your advances.

HARDCASTLE. And yet he might have seen something in me above a common innkeeper, too.

SIR CHARLES. Yes, Dick, but he mistook you for an uncommon innkeeper, ha! ha! ha!

HARDCASTLE. Well, I'm in too good spirits to think of anything but joy. Yes, my dear friend, this union of our families will make our personal friendships *hereditary*; and though my daughter's fortune is but small—

SIR CHARLES. Why, Dick, will you talk of fortune to me? My son is possessed of more than a competence already, and can want nothing but a good and virtuous girl to share his happiness and increase it. If they like each other, as you say they do—

HARDCASTLE. *If*, man! I tell you they *do* like each other. My daughter as good as told me so.

SIR CHARLES. But girls are apt to flatter themselves, you know.

HARDCASTLE. I saw him grasp her hand in the warmest manner myself; and here he comes to put you out of your *ifs*, I warrant him.

Enter Marlow.

MARLOW. I come, sir, once more, to ask pardon for my strange conduct. I can scarce reflect on my insolence without confusion.

HARDCASTLE. Tut, boy, a trifle. You take it too gravely. An hour or two's laughing with my daughter will set all to rights again. She'll never like you the worse for it.

MARLOW. Sir, I shall be always proud of her approbation.

HARDCASTLE. Approbation is but a cold word, Mr.

Marlow; if I am not deceived, you have something more than approbation thereabouts. You take me?

MARLOW. Really, sir, I have not that happiness.

HARDCASTLE. Come, boy, I'm an old fellow, and know what's what, as well as you that are younger. I know what has past between you; but mum.

MARLOW. Sure, sir, nothing has passed between us but the most profound respect on my side, and the most distant reserve on hers. You don't think, sir, that my impudence has been passed upon all the rest of the family.

HARDCASTLE. Impudence! No, I don't say that—not quite impudence—though girls like to be played with, and rumpled a little too, sometimes. But she has told no tales, I assure you.

MARLOW. I never gave her the slightest cause.

HARDCASTLE. Well, well, I like modesty in its place well enough. But this is overacting, young gentleman. You may be open. Your father and I will like you the better for it.

MARLOW. May I die, sir, if I ever—

HARDCASTLE. I tell you, she don't dislike you; and as I'm sure you like her—

MARLOW. Dear sir—I protest, sir—

HARDCASTLE. I see no reason why you should not be joined as fast as the parson can tie you.

MARLOW. But hear me, sir—

HARDCASTLE. Your father approves the match, I admire it, every moment's delay will be doing mischief; so—

MARLOW. But why won't you hear me? By all that's just and true, I never gave Miss Hardcastle the slightest mark of my attachment, or even the most distant hint to suspect me of affection. We had but one interview, and that was formal, modest, and uninteresting.

HARDCASTLE (*aside*). This fellow's formal, modest impudence is beyond bearing.

SIR CHARLES. And you never grasped her hand, or made any protestations!

MARLOW. As heaven is my witness, I came down in obedience to your commands. I saw the lady without emotion, and parted without reluctance. I hope you'll exact no further proofs of my duty, nor prevent me from leaving a house in which I suffer so many **mortifications**.　　　　*Exit*.

SIR CHARLES. I'm astonished at the air of sincerity with which he parted.

HARDCASTLE. And I'm astonished at the deliberate intrepidity of his assurance.

SIR CHARLES. I dare pledge my life and honor upon his truth.

HARDCASTLE (*looking out to right*). Here comes my daughter, and I would stake my happiness upon her veracity.

Enter Miss Hardcastle.

HARDCASTLE. Kate, come hither, child. Answer us sincerely, and without reserve; has Mr. Marlow made you any professions of love and affection?

MISS HARDCASTLE. The question is very abrupt,

---

mortifications: humiliations or embarrassments

sir! But since you require unreserved sincerity, I think he has.

HARDCASTLE *(to* Sir Charles). You see.

SIR CHARLES. And pray, madam, have you and my son had more than one interview?

MISS HARDCASTLE. Yes, sir, several.

HARDCASTLE *(to* Sir Charles). You see.

SIR CHARLES. But did he profess any attachment?

MISS HARDCASTLE. A lasting one.

SIR CHARLES. Did he talk of love?

MISS HARDCASTLE. Much, sir.

SIR CHARLES. Amazing! And all this formally?

MISS HARDCASTLE. Formally.

HARDCASTLE. Now, my friend, I hope you are satisfied.

SIR CHARLES. And how did he behave, madam?

MISS HARDCASTLE. As most professed admirers do. Said some civil things of my face, talked much of his want of merit, and the greatness of mine; mentioned his heart, gave a short tragedy speech, and ended with pretended rapture.

SIR CHARLES. Now I'm perfectly convinced, indeed. I know his conversation among women to be modest and *submissive.* This forward, *canting, ranting* manner by no means describes him, and I am confident he never sat for the picture.

MISS HARDCASTLE. Then what, sir, if I should convince you to your face of my sincerity? If you and my papa, in about half an hour, will place yourselves behind that screen, you shall hear him declare his passion to me in person.

SIR CHARLES. Agreed. And if I find him what you

describe, all my happiness in him must have an end.   *Exit.*

MISS HARDCASTLE. And if you don't find him what I describe—I fear my happiness must never have a beginning.

                Exeunt.

[Scene II:] Scene changes to the back of the garden.

Enter Hastings.

HASTINGS. What an idiot am I, to wait here for a fellow, who probably takes a delight in mortifying me. He never intended to be punctual, and I'll wait no longer. What do I see? It is he, and perhaps with news of my Constance.

Enter Tony, *booted and spattered.*

HASTINGS. My honest squire! I now find you a man of your word. This looks like friendship.

TONY. Aye, I'm your friend, and the best friend you have in the world, if you knew but all. This riding by night, by the bye, is cursedly tiresome. It has shook me worse than the basket of a stage-coach.

HASTINGS. But how? Where did you leave your fellow travelers? Are they in safety? Are they housed?

TONY. Five and twenty miles in two hours and a half is no such bad driving. The poor beasts have **smoked** for it: rabbit me, but I'd rather ride forty miles after a fox, than ten with such **varment.**

HASTINGS. Well, but where have you left the ladies? I die with impatience.

TONY. Left them? Why, where should I leave them, but where I found them?

HASTINGS. This is a riddle.

TONY. Riddle me this, then. What's that goes round the house, and round the house, and never touches the house?

HASTINGS. I'm still astray.

TONY. Why, that's it, mon. I have led them astray. By jingo, there's not a pond or slough within five miles of the place but they can tell the taste of.

HASTINGS. Ha, ha, ha, I understand; you took them in a round, while they supposed themselves going forward. And so you have at last brought them home again.

TONY. You shall hear. I first took them down Feather-Bed Lane, where we stuck fast in the mud. I then rattled them crack over the stones of Up-and-Down Hill—I then introduced them to the gibbet on Heavy-Tree Heath, and from that, with a **circumbendibus,** I fairly lodged them in the horse-pond at the bottom of the garden.

---

smoked: sweated or steamed up as a result of the frantic driving

varment: objectionable animals or people

circumbendibus: Tony uses a humorous, Latin-sounding word to describe the roundabout trip.

HASTINGS. But no accident, I hope.

TONY. No, no. Only mother is confoundedly frightened. She thinks herself forty miles off. She's sick of the journey, and the cattle can scarce crawl. So, if your own horses be ready, you may whip off with cousin, and I'll be bound that no soul here can budge a foot to follow you.

HASTINGS. My dear friend, how can I be grateful?

TONY. Aye, now it's dear friend, noble squire. Just now, it was all idiot, cub, and run me through the guts. Damn *your* way of fighting, I say. After we take a knock in this part of the country, we kiss and be friends. But if you had run me through the guts, then I should be dead, and you might go kiss the hangman.

HASTINGS. The rebuke is just. But I must hasten to relieve Miss Neville; if you keep the old lady employed, I promise to take care of the young one.

TONY. Never fear me. Here she comes. Vanish. [*Exit* Hastings.] She's got from the pond, and draggled up to the waist like a mermaid.

Enter Mrs. Hardcastle.

MRS. HARDCASTLE. Oh, Tony, I'm killed. Shook. Battered to death. I shall never survive it. That last jolt that laid us against the quickset hedge has done my business.

TONY. Alack, mamma, it was all your own fault. You would be running away by night, without knowing one inch of the way.

MRS. HARDCASTLE. I wish we were at home again.

I never met so many accidents in so short a journey. Drenched in the mud, overturned in a ditch, stuck fast in a slough, jolted to a jelly, and at last to lose our way. Whereabouts do you think we are, Tony?

TONY. By my guess we should be upon Crackskull Common, about forty miles from home.

MRS. HARDCASTLE. O lud! O lud! the most notorious spot in all the country. We only want a robbery to make a complete night on't.

TONY. Don't be afraid, mamma, don't be afraid. Two of the five that **kept here** are hanged, and the other three may not find us. Don't be afraid. Is that a man that's galloping behind us? No; it's only a tree. Don't be afraid.

MRS. HARDCASTLE. The fright will certainly kill me.

TONY. Do you see any thing like a black hat moving behind the thicket?

MRS. HARDCASTLE. O death!

TONY. No, it's only a cow. Don't be afraid, mamma, don't be afraid.

MRS. HARDCASTLE. As I'm alive, Tony, I see a man coming towards us. Ah! I'm sure on't. If he perceives us, we are undone.

TONY *(aside)*. Father-in-law, by all that's unlucky, come to take one of his night walks. *(To her.)* Ah, it's a highwayman, with pistols as long as my arm. A damned ill-looking fellow.

MRS. HARDCASTLE. Good Heaven defend us! He approaches.

----

kept here: that used to stay around here

Tony. Do you hide yourself in that thicket and leave me to manage him. If there be any danger I'll cough and cry hem. When I cough be sure to keep close.

Mrs. Hardcastle *hides behind a tree in the back scene.*

Enter Hardcastle.

Hardcastle. I'm mistaken, or I heard voices of people in want of help. Oh, Tony, is that you? I did not expect you so soon back. Are your mother and her charge in safety?

Tony. Very safe, sir, at my Aunt Pedigree's. Hem.

Mrs. Hardcastle *(from behind).* Ah, death! I find there's danger.

Hardcastle. Forty miles in three hours; sure, that's too much, my youngster.

Tony. Stout horses and willing minds make short journeys, as they say. Hem.

Mrs. Hardcastle *(from behind).* Sure he'll do the dear boy no harm.

Hardcastle. But I heard a voice here; I should be glad to know from whence it came?

Tony. It was I, sir, talking to myself, sir. I was saying that forty miles in four hours was very good going. Hem. As to be sure it was. Hem. I have got a sort of cold by being out in the air. We'll go in if you please. Hem.

Hardcastle. But if you talked to yourself, you did not answer yourself. I am certain I heard two voices, and am resolved *(raising his voice)* to find the other out.

MRS. HARDCASTLE *(from behind)*. Oh! he's coming to find me out. Oh!

TONY. What need you go, sir, if I tell you? Hem. I'll lay down my life for the truth—hem—I'll tell you all, sir. *(Detaining him.)*

HARDCASTLE. I tell you I will not be detained. I insist on seeing. It's in vain to expect I'll believe you.

MRS. HARDCASTLE *(running forward from behind)*. O lud, he'll murder my poor boy, my darling. Here, good gentleman, whet your rage upon me. Take my money, my life, but spare that young gentleman, spare my child, if you have any mercy.

HARDCASTLE. My wife! as I'm a Christian. From whence can she come, or what does she mean?

MRS. HARDCASTLE *(kneeling)*. Take compassion on us, good Mr. Highwayman. Take our money, our watches, all we have, but spare our lives. We will never bring you to justice, indeed, we won't, good Mr. Highwayman.

HARDCASTLE. I believe the woman's out of her senses. What, Dorothy, don't you know me?

MRS. HARDCASTLE. Mr. Hardcastle, as I'm alive! My fears blinded me. But who, my dear, could have expected to meet you here, in this frightful place, so far from home. What has brought you to follow us?

HARDCASTLE. Sure, Dorothy, you have not lost your wits. So far from home, when you are within forty yards of your own door! *(To him.)* This is one of your old tricks, you graceless rogue, you! *(To her.)* Don't you know the gate, and the mulberry tree; and don't you remember the horsepond, my dear?

MRS. HARDCASTLE. Yes, I shall remember the horsepond as long as I live; I have caught my death in it. *(To Tony.)* And it is to you, you graceless varlet, I owe all this? I'll teach you to abuse your mother, I will.

TONY. Ecod, mother, all the parish says you have spoiled me, and so you may take the fruits on't.

MRS. HARDCASTLE. I'll spoil you, I will. *(Follows him off the stage.)*

HARDCASTLE. There's morality, however, in his reply.   *Exit.*

Enter Hastings *and* Miss Neville.

HASTINGS. My dear Constance, why will you deliberate thus? If we delay a moment, all is lost forever. Pluck up a little resolution, and we shall soon be out of the reach of her *malignity*.

MISS NEVILLE. I find it impossible. My spirits are so sunk with the agitations I have suffered, that I am unable to face any new danger. Two or three years' patience will at last crown us with happiness.

HASTINGS. Such a tedious delay is worse than inconstancy. Let us fly, my charmer. Let us date our happiness from this very moment. Perish fortune. Love and content will increase what we possess beyond a monarch's revenue. Let me prevail.

MISS NEVILLE. No, Mr. Hastings, no. Prudence once more comes to my relief, and I will obey its dictates. In the moment of passion, fortune may be despised, but it ever produces a lasting repentance. I'm resolved to apply to Mr. Hardcastle's compassion and justice for redress.

HASTINGS. But though he had the will, he has not the power to relieve you.

MISS NEVILLE. But he has influence, and upon that I am resolved to rely.

HASTINGS. I have no hopes. But since you persist, I must reluctantly obey you.   *Exeunt.*

Scene III: Scene changes [the house.]

Enter Sir Charles *and* Miss Hardcastle.

SIR CHARLES. What a situation am I in. If what you say appears, I shall then find a guilty son. If what he says be true, I shall then lose one that, of all others, I most wished for a daughter.

MISS HARDCASTLE. I am proud of your approbation, and, to show I merit it, if you place yourselves as I directed, you shall hear his explicit declaration. But he comes.

SIR CHARLES. I'll to your father, and keep him to the appointment.   *Exit* Sir Charles.

Enter Marlow.

MARLOW. Though prepared for setting out, I come once more to take leave, nor did I, till this moment, know the pain I feel in the separation.

MISS HARDCASTLE (*in her own natural manner*). I believe sufferings cannot be very great, sir, which you can so easily remove. A day or two longer, perhaps, might lessen your uneasiness, by showing the little value of what you think proper to regret.

MARLOW (*aside*). This girl every moment improves upon me. (To her.) It must not be, madam. I have already trifled too long with my heart. My very pride begins to submit to my passion. The disparity of education and fortune, the anger of a parent, and the contempt of my equals begin to lose their weight; and nothing can restore me to myself but this painful effort of resolution.

MISS HARDCASTLE. Then go, sir. I'll urge nothing more to detain you. Though my family be as good as hers you came down to visit, and my education, I hope, not inferior, what are these advantages without equal affluence? I must remain contented with the slight approbation of imputed merit; I must have only the mockery of your addresses, while all your serious aims are fixed on fortune.

Enter Hardcastle *and* Sir Charles *from behind.*

SIR CHARLES. Here, behind this screen.

HARDCASTLE. Aye, aye, make no noise. I'll engage my Kate covers him with confusion at last.

MARLOW. By heavens, madam, fortune was ever my smallest consideration. Your beauty at first caught my eye; for who could see that without emotion? But every moment that I converse with you, steals in some new grace, heightens the picture, and gives it stronger expression. What at first seemed rustic plainness, now appears refined simplicity. What seemed forward assurance, now strikes me as the result of courageous innocence and conscious virtue.

SIR CHARLES. What can it mean! He amazes me!

HARDCASTLE. I told you how it would be. Hush!

MARLOW. I am now determined to stay, madam, and I have too good an opinion of my father's discernment, when he sees you, to doubt his approbation.

MISS HARDCASTLE. No, Mr. Marlow, I will not, cannot detain you. Do you think I could suffer a connection, in which there is the smallest room for repentance? Do you think I would take the mean advantage of a *transient* passion, to load you with confusion? Do you think I could ever relish that happiness, which was acquired by lessening yours!

MARLOW. By all that's good, I can have no happiness but what's in your power to grant me. Nor shall I ever feel repentance, but in not having seen your merits before. I will stay, even contrary to your wishes; and though you should persist to shun me, I will make my respectful assiduities atone for the levity of my past conduct.

MISS HARDCASTLE. Sir, I must entreat you'll desist. As our acquaintance began, so let it end, in indifference. I might have given an hour or two to levity; but, seriously. Mr. Marlow, do you think I could ever submit to a connection, where *I* must appear mercenary, and *you* imprudent? Do you think, I could ever catch at the confident addresses of a secure admirer?

MARLOW (*kneeling*). Does this look like security? Does this look like confidence? No, madam, every moment that shows me your merit, only serves to increase my diffidence and confusion. Here let me continue—

SIR CHARLES. I can hold it no longer. Charles, Charles, how hast thou deceived me! Is this your indifference, your uninteresting conversation!

HARDCASTLE. Your cold contempt; your formal interview. What have you to say now?

MARLOW. That I'm all amazement! What can it mean?

HARDCASTLE. It means that you can say and unsay things at pleasure; that you can address a lady in private, and deny it in public; that you have one story for us, and another for my daughter!

MARLOW. Daughter! This lady your daughter!

HARDCASTLE. Yes, sir, my only daughter, my Kate; whose else should she be?

MARLOW. Oh, the devil!

MISS HARDCASTLE. Yes, sir, that very identical tall, squinting lady you were pleased to take me for. (*Curtsying.*) She that you addressed as the mild, modest, sentimental man of gravity, and the bold, forward, agreeable Rattle of the Ladies' Club: ha, ha, ha.

MARLOW. Zounds, there's no bearing this; it's worse than death.

MISS HARDCASTLE. In which of your characters, sir, will you give us leave to address you? As the faltering gentleman, with looks on the ground, that speaks just to be heard, and hates hypocrisy: or the loud, confident creature, that keeps it up with Mrs. Mantrap, and old Miss Biddy Buckskin, till three in the morning? Ha, ha, ha!

MARLOW. Oh, curse on my noisy head. I never attempted to be impudent yet, that I was not taken down. I must be gone.

HARDCASTLE. By the hand of my body, but you shall not. I see it was all a mistake, and I am rejoiced to find it. You shall not, sir, I tell you. I know she'll forgive you. Won't you forgive him, Kate? We'll all forgive you. Take courage, man. *(They retire, she tormenting him, to the back scene.)*

Enter Mrs. Hardcastle *and* Tony.

MRS. HARDCASTLE. So, so, they're gone off. Let them go, I care not.

HARDCASTLE. Who gone?

MRS. HARDCASTLE. My dutiful niece and her gentleman, Mr. Hastings, from town. He who came down with our modest visitor here.

SIR CHARLES. Who, my honest George Hastings? As worthy a fellow as lives, and the girl could not have made a more prudent choice.

HARDCASTLE. Then, by the hand of my body, I'm proud of the connection.

MRS. HARDCASTLE. Well, if he has taken away the lady, he has not taken her fortune; that remains in this family to console us for her loss.

HARDCASTLE. Sure, Dorothy, you would not be so mercenary?

MRS. HARDCASTLE. Aye, that's my affair, not yours.

HARDCASTLE. But you know, if your son, when of age, refuses to marry his cousin, her whole fortune is then at her own disposal.

MRS. HARDCASTLE. Ah, but he's not of age, and she has not thought proper to wait for his refusal.

Enter Hastings *and* Miss Neville.

MRS. HARDCASTLE (*aside*). What, returned so soon! I begin not to like it.

HASTINGS (*to* Hardcastle). For my late attempt to fly off with your niece, let my present confusion be my punishment. We are now come back, to appeal from your justice to your humanity. By her father's consent, I first paid her my addresses, and our passions were first founded in duty.

MISS NEVILLE. Since his death, I have been obliged to stoop to *dissimulation* to avoid oppression. In an hour of levity, I was ready even to give up my fortune to secure my choice. But I'm now recovered from the delusion, and hope from your tenderness what is denied me from a nearer connection.

MRS. HARDCASTLE. Pshaw, pshaw, this is all but the whining end of a modern novel.

HARDCASTLE. Be it what it will, I'm glad they're

come back to reclaim their due. Come hither, Tony, boy. Do you refuse this lady's hand whom I now offer you?

TONY. What signifies my refusing? You know I can't refuse her till I'm of age, father.

HARDCASTLE. While I thought concealing your age, boy, was likely to *conduce* to your improvement, I concurred with your mother's desire to keep it secret. But since I find she turns it to a wrong use, I must now declare, you have been of age these three months.

TONY. Of age! Am I of age, father?

HARDCASTLE. Above three months.

TONY. Then you'll see the first use I'll make of my liberty. (*Taking* Miss Neville's *hand.*) Witness all men by these presents, that I, Anthony Lumpkin, Esquire, of BLANK place, refuse you, Constantia Neville, spinster, of no place at all, for my true and lawful wife. So Constance Neville may marry whom she pleases and Tony Lumpkin is his own man again!

SIR CHARLES. O brave squire!

HASTINGS. My worthy friend!

MRS. HARDCASTLE. My undutiful offspring!

MARLOW. Joy, my dear George, I give you joy, sincerely. And could I prevail upon my little tyrant here to be less arbitrary, I should be the happiest man alive, if you would return me the favor.

HASTINGS (*to* Miss Hardcastle). Come, madam, you are now driven to the very last scene of all your contrivances. I know you like him, I'm sure he loves you, and you must and shall have him.

HARDCASTLE *(joining their hands)*. And I say so, too. And Mr. Marlow, if she makes as good a wife as she has a daughter, I don't believe you'll ever repent your bargain. So now to supper. Tomorrow we shall gather all the poor of the parish about us, and the mistakes of the night shall be crowned with a merry morning; so, boy, take her; and as you have been mistaken in the mistress, my wish is, that you may never be mistaken in the wife.

Epilogue

By Dr. Goldsmith

WELL, having stooped to conquer with success,
And gained a husband without aid from dress,
Still as a barmaid, I could wish it too,
As I have conquered him to conquer you:
And let me say, for all your resolution,
That pretty barmaids have done execution.
Our life is all a play, composed to please,
"We have our exits and our entrances."
The first act shows the simple country maid,
Harmless and young, of everything afraid;
Blushes when hired, and with unmeaning action,
"I hopes as how to give you satisfaction."
Her second act displays a livelier scene,—
Th' unblushing barmaid of a country inn,
Who whisks about the house, at market caters,
Talks loud, coquets the guests, and scolds the
    waiters.
Next the scene shifts to town, and there she soars,
The **chophouse toast** of ogling connoisseurs.

"We have our exits and our entrances": a parody of Shakespeare's line from *As You Like It*, Act II, scene vii, l. 141. The rest of the epilogue carries through the figure of speech.

chophouse toast: The barmaid has become sophisticated and is the toast of the admiring diners.

On squires and **cits** she there displays her arts,
And on the gridiron broils her lovers' hearts—
And as she smiles, her triumphs to complete,
Even common councilmen forget to eat.
The fourth act shows her wedded to the squire,
And madam now begins to hold it higher;
Pretends to taste, at operas cries **caro,**
And quits her **"Nancy Dawson,"** for **Che Faro.**
Dotes upon dancing, and in all her pride,
Swims round the room, the **Heinel** of Cheapside:
Ogles and leers with artificial skill,
Till having lost in age the power to kill,
She sits all night at cards, and ogles at **spadille.**
Such, through our lives, th' eventful history—
The fifth and last act still remains for me.
The barmaid now for your protection prays,
Turns female barrister, and pleads for **Bayes.**

---

cits: citizens, the ordinary people
caro: Italian for "dear one" or "beloved"; a shout of praise for an artistic performance
"Nancy Dawson": then, a popular song
Che Faro: an aria from *Orfeo* (1762), an opera by Christoph Willibald Glück, which the barmaid now sings instead of "pop" songs
Heinel: "Madame" Anna Heinel was a German dancer popular with the fashionable set.
spadille: the ace of spades in the old card game called ombre
Bayes: Dr. Goldsmith identifies himself here with Bayes, a character (an amateur author) in the play *The Rehearsal* (1671), written by George Villiers, Second Duke of Buckingham, and some collaborators.